THE
MYTHOLOGY
OF SCIENCE

ROUSAS JOHN
RUSHDOONY

VALLECITO, CALIFORNIA

Ross House Books
PO Box 67
Vallecito, CA 95251

Library of Congress Control Number: 2001117783
ISBN: 1-879998-26-2

Printed in the United States of America

The reprinting of this volume
was made possible
by the generous and faithful support of
of Ivan R. Bierly.

Other books by
Rousas John Rushdoony

The Institutes of Biblical Law, Vol. I
The Institutes of Biblical Law, Vol. II, Law & Society
The Institutes of Biblical Law, Vol. III, The Intent of the Law
Systematic Theology (2 volumes)
Hebrews, James & Jude
The Gospel of John
Romans & Galatians
Thy Kingdom Come
This Independent Republic
Foundations of Social Order
The "Atheism" of the Early Church
The Biblical Philosophy of History
The Messianic Character of American Education
The Philosophy of the Christian Curriculum
Christianity and the State
Salvation and Godly Rule
God's Plan for Victory
Politics of Guilt and Pity
Roots of Reconstruction
The One and the Many
Revolt Against Maturity
By What Standard?
Law & Liberty

For a complete listing of available books
by Rousas John Rushdoony and other
Christian reconstructionists, contact:

ROSS HOUSE BOOKS
PO Box 67
Vallecito, CA 95251

Table of Contents

Foreword to the 2001 printing

by Mark R. Rushdoony

One might think it odd to republish a book on science that is one-third of a century old without an extensive rewrite using current bibliographical sources. *The Mythology of Science*, however, is not a book on science in the empirical sense of observation and quantification. Its purpose, in fact, is to point out the fraud of the empirical claims of much modern science since Charles Darwin. This book is about the religious nature of evolutionary thought and how these religious presuppositions underlay our modern intellectual paradigm, and are deferred to as sacrosanct by institutions and disciplines far removed from the empirical sciences.

This book was first published in 1967, at the height of the U.S.-Soviet "space race." The bibliographical data of this book is dated; its analyses are not. In fact, the author's analysis in the midst of a virtual cult of science is more penetrating for its prescient understanding of the direction of science divorced from the reality of an Omnipotent God:

> Thus it is not predestination in itself which is an offense to man, but predestination *by God*. The culmination of process is control by scientific man of the various aspects and phases of process, so that evolution is to be guided and

1

controlled, life is to be created, minds invented as tools of the new gods, human minds shaped and directed by the gods of science through chemistry, and society itself made into a great machine in which man, economics, education, sexual reproduction and all else are made subservient to predestination by scientific controllers.

The author's comments must also be viewed as particularly courageous in light of the deferential awe of science and all things "scientific" at the time. This prevailing deference, as the author notes, extended so far into the church that few wished to consider the possibility that Scripture did not allow for an evolutionary interpretation. The fear of being characterized as "unscientific" caused most churches to abandon Biblical Creationism without a fight. The humiliation of William Jennings Bryan by Clarence Darrow over a generation earlier had led to a near-total retreat of the church from any confrontation with evolutionary thought. The book reviews have also been retained as appendices. They were reviews of already dated books at the time of this work's first publication. They are of value as comment on ostensibly conservative, liberal, and Catholic stands on evolution. The sole change from the author's manuscript has been to the title of chapter three. The original title, "Man in 1984," had an appropriately futuristic ring to it in 1967. Its title has been changed to "Orwell's 1984: Horror or Hope?" to reflect the religious, ethical divide that continues to shape the debate. Again, the author's insight remains as relevant today as ever:

> The world of 1984, however, is the old world of Satan, of the fall of man.... the old world of the tower of Babel, perpetually doomed to confusion, destruction, and scattering.... It is no brave new world but the age-old doomed world of covenant-breaking man.... The world of 1984 shall be God's world, and man in 1984 shall be only what the predestinating power and control of God intend him to be ....

The "mythology" of modern science is its religious devotion to the myth of evolution. Evolution "so expresses or coincides with the contemporary spirit that its often radical contradictions and absurdities are never apparent, in that they express the basic presuppositions, however untenable, of everyday life and thought." In evolution, man is the highest expression of intelligence and reason, and such thinking will not yield itself to submission to a God it views as a human cultural creation, useful, if at all, only in a cultural context.

Even by the rationalism that receives its justification in evolution, origins of matter and life cannot be subject to the empirical method. It is history, and is no longer observable, measurable, or repeatable. Views of origins are dependent on faith, and one's position speaks much as to one's religious tenets. Each faith will seek to exclude the other, for the faiths are mutually exclusive. Thus evolution allows, if perhaps reluctantly, for ideas of animal rights and various pantheistic returns to the worship of "nature" because such thinking is naturalistic and not at variance with the underlying faith in natural causation. Evolutionary faith, however, cannot tolerate any view of the natural world or science that places it under another faith, such as the Christian belief in a sovereign causative God. "Darwin therefore met," says the author, "not a scientific need, but a religious hunger." Darwin gave an ostensibly scientific justification for man's rebellion against God. He put men at the top of the evolutionary ladder, allowing them to believe they had realized Satan's lure to Adam and Eve and become "as gods, knowing [determining] good and evil" (Genesis 3:5).

It is worth noting that the mechanism for evolution proposed by Darwin, natural selection, has long been dismissed as incapable of producing the changes evolution necessitates. Likewise, as the author points out, Freud's reliance on Lamarck's discredited theory of acquired characteristics is an embarrassment to modern psychoanalysis. The failure of the hard science of Darwin and Freud did not change much. Their evolutionary theories remained after their proposed mechanisms were discredited. Regularly a new "scientific" explanation merely replaces the old. The theory remains because the faith that trusted in it made it "an axiomatic truth to the age" and a "criterion for judging and assessing reality."

We can attack the science of evolution all we want, but the battle for our faith, true science, and our culture is a religious one over the nature of truth. Evolution is a religious faith that has become entrenched as a presupposition of modern thought. For Christians to argue about the "unproven" nature of the evolutionary hypothesis or the circular reasoning of its thought is of some value, but the essential issue is that two opposing religious faiths are in conflict. Evolution is popular because it is such a useful paradigm to sinful men; it dispenses with God as a prerequisite of all things. But Christianity as a religious faith depends not on proofs that are constructs of man's fallen mind, but on the reality of an almighty God who reveals Himself to us by grace. Christianity, too, depends on circular reasoning; we begin and end with faith in God and His revelation. The basis of science and all other thought will ultimately be found in a higher ethical and philosophical context; whether or not this is seen as religious does not change the nature of that context. Ultimately, the great questions of life and thought are of faith; they involve saying, "This is my starting point; this is what I believe to be true." Part of the mythology of modern evolutionary science is its failure to admit that it is a faith-based paradigm.

The purpose of this book in 1967 was to define the nature of the opposing religious systems of thought, Christian creationism and Darwinism (in its various forms). It was a call to urge Christians to stand firm for Biblical six-day creationism as a fundamental aspect of their faith in the Creator. This need still exists, hence the republication of this book.

Mark R. Rushdoony
May 21, 2001

Chapter One

The Mythology of Science

On the surface, a *myth* is the illusion of an age or a culture whereby life and its origins are interpreted. As such, the myth has an axiomatic truth to the age and is its criterion for judging and assessing reality.

But much more is involved in the concept of *myth*. A myth is the attempt of a culture to overcome history, to negate the forces and ravages of time, and to make the universe amenable and subject to man. The myth reveals a hatred of history. History shows movement in terms of forces beyond man and in judgment over man; history rides heavily over man, is inescapably ethical, shows a continuing conflict between good and evil, and clearly reveals man as the actor, not the playwright and director. And this man hates. To fill a role he never wrote, to enter on stage at a time not of his choosing, this man resents. The purpose man then sets for himself in his myths is *to end history*, to make man the absolute governor by decreeing an end to the movement that is history. Where his myths acknowledge man's lot in history, man ascribes his sorry role, not to his depravity, but to jealousy of the gods. The goal of the myth, ever more clearly enunciated over time, has become the destruction of history and the enthronement of man as the new governor of the universe.

The *means* used by man to accomplish the goal of his myth is *magic*. The purpose of magic is the total control by man over man, nature, and the supernatural. Whatever the form magic takes, this is its goal. The relationship of magic is therefore basically to science rather than to Biblical religion. Under the influence of Christianity, science escaped the constraints of magic. The purpose of science gradually ceased to be an attempt to play god and became rather the exercise of dominion over the earth under God. The redeemed Christian is God's vicegerent over the earth, and science is one of man's tools in establishing and furthering that dominion. For science to overstep that role is to forsake science for magic. The purposes of modern science are increasingly those of magic, the exercise of total control. The essential goal of modern science is knowledge in order to have *prediction, planning, and control*. Thus magic has again triumphed, and modern science is popular precisely because man today, wedded again to the world of myth, demands magic to overcome history, to eliminate the ethical struggle and to place man beyond good and evil and beyond judgment. On the whole, modern science has taken readily to this new role, and it is enjoying its status as magician in the mind of modern man. Science has become magic and is governed by myth.

Basic to God's nature as sovereign is His omnipotence. It is not only an assertion of the Bible, but also a basic presupposition of every page, that all things are possible with God, and with Him nothing is impossible. It is not surprising that man, having succumbed to the lure of myth and believing himself to be his own god, should proceed on the premise that all things are possible with man, scientific man.

The examples of this faith are many and striking. The world of history condemns the sun to death. The sun was created, and therefore the sun can die. It is not eternal nor any does it have self-regenerative power enabling it to revive itself at will. The sun has a history; it moves in terms of a predetermined and predestined plan not its own. The sun, like the entire universe, and man included, belongs to the world of history. It must die. But man the myth-maker wants a world refashioned according to his own imagination, created by his own word. History must therefore either be arrested, or, having run its course, be recreated by the new god, the new great magician, scientific man. Thus Kenneth Heuer, a specialist in planetary astronomy, and a fellow of Britain's Royal Astronomical Society, has written, in discussing the death of the sun:

> Still another possibility would be to construct our own sun, a source of heat and light which might be suspended in the sky and hold the hovering demons of cold and darkness at bay. This artificial sun would operate by subatomic energy. In the remaining years of grace, man might learn how to run the carbon cycle. Hydrogen, the fuel, is abundant, and other light atoms, such as lithium, are also plentiful sources of energy. With several billions of years of time at his disposal for research, man should be able to develop cheap, abundant, and manageable subatomic power.[1]

If fifty billion years is too long to wait, we can be comforted by the headline writer who informs us that a great future is reasonably close: "Workless World Foreseen By Scientist." Dr. Glenn T. Seaborg, atomic scientist who heads the United States Atomic Energy Commission, spoke of the new world being created by science:

> These systems promise us a way of life that is entirely different from anything man has ever imagined.
>
> Up to now work—labor, employment or simply occupation—has been a central notion of human existence.
>
> There always have been a few people who live well doing nothing, but the idea of almost an entire civilization living well, with essentially no one physically working, is almost inconceivable to us.

---

[1] Kenneth Heuer, "The End of the World," *Panorama, The Laurel Review*, no. 1 (December 1957), 83. Adapted from Heuer's chapt. 5 of *The Next Fifty Billion Years* (Viking Press, 1957).

"Fortunately," Dr. Seaborg adds, this time is not yet here, because, as one of the new gods and judges, he feels most men are not ready for paradise. (In God's paradise, man worked, but there was no curse on his work.) Seaborg also protects himself by virtually denying his statement: "All that may change in a 'workless world' is our definition or connotation of the word 'work.'"[2] Such statements by Seaborg, as well as by Heuer, are read with simple faith by the members of modern society; they believe in the mythology of science.

Scientists are self-consciously asserting that they are in the vanguard of a new renaissance. Dr. Caryl P. Haskins, president of the Carnegie Institution of Washington and a member of the Yale Corporation, has written, "It may be no accident that the emergence of science in its modern form occurred contemporaneously with the Renaissance revolution in political thought and action. And it is that heritage of which the philosophy and methods—not primarily the practical results—of American science must be an important guardian in our nation today." Haskins sees science as possessing an unusual role in the development and formation of the future. "Indeed, a striking characteristic of the body of scientific knowledge is the degree to which, in organization and growth, it recalls a developing organism, or, on a larger scale, an evolving population of organisms. Like the society that supports it, the body of science is, in something more than a purely allegorical sense, a living thing."[3] If "the body of science is, in something more than a purely allegorical sense, a living thing," what is this new "living thing" which now shapes man and the future, the new god of the universe?

Another scientist, Dr. Franklin Murphy, Chancellor of the University of California at Los Angeles, believes that we are now witnessing "the return of Renaissance Man" as a result of "the scientific revolution." However, he regards it as "more of

---

[2] William J. Perkinson, "Workless World Foreseen by Scientist," Santa Ana, California, *The Register*, 12 December 1966, B10.

[3] Caryl P. Haskins, "Two Faces of Science," in *Ventures*, Magazine of the Yale Graduate School, vol. VI, no. 2 (Fall 1966): 23.

a revolution than a renaissance because it has very few roots in the past, unlike the Italian renaissance. It's mainly pointed toward the present and the future. It has few historical benchmarks." The evidences of this revolution are many. The arts reveal it clearly in the willingness of man to "cast aside his prejudices in terms of what his ears and eyes have been accustomed to hearing and seeing and begin to examine the arts, himself and his society with the same degree of freedom which he has given in the past to chemistry and physics. The arts cannot remain immune to the tremendous revolutionary ferment generated by the scientific revolution."[4]

Dr. Murphy saw "three major inputs" behind this new renaissance or revolution:

> I list three major inputs....First is the death of Calvinism, that set of traditions which said that to live richly in one's emotional life is a dishonorable thing for a man to do.

> Secondly...the impact of the scientific revolution. It's shaking up everybody's confidence that there are any timeless verities. It's leading to an acceptance of experimentation. That's almost the name of the current game.

> The third input is the growth of a new open-mindedness, a willingness to look candidly at the old prejudices, which we find today in our entire society.

> All of this is producing what you may call a Renaissance Man...what some have called a "man for many seasons."

> Of course, he is not being born without a certain amount of friction.

> People are having a hard time understanding, for instance, the reluctance of the Supreme Court to restrict freedom of expression by rigid definitions of what is "obscenity."

> The court is doing no more than respecting the principles of free speech as written into the U.S. Constitution.[5]

---

4. John Bryan, "Franklin Murphy on the Return of Renaissance Man," in the Los Angeles *Herald-Examiner California Living*, 11 December 1966, 6.
5. *Ibid.*

Dr. Murphy's three "inputs" are basically one, and his statement lacks honesty. Calvinism never held that "to live richly in one's emotional life is a dishonorable thing for a man to do." On the contrary, this attitude, in America, came with Unitarianism and Transcendentalism, both anti-Calvinistic movements. Calvinism is a term Murphy uses as a euphemism for and evasion of the reality of Biblical Christianity, for it would be more open and controversial to ascribe this "dishonorable" attitude to Christianity. For Murphy Calvinism means the idea of any absolute, supernatural law of God. His second "input" says the same thing: "timeless verities," absolute truth, a real right and wrong, good and evil, have been dropped in favor of "the current game... experimentation." Murphy's "third input" is men's willingness to accept this scientific revolution against God. There is therefore for Murphy a "renaissance," a "rebirth" of man because there is no longer an moral and religious law over man. Man, scientific man, has become his own god.

The use of the term *renaissance* is thus significant, even with the qualifications. The Renaissance revived pagan humanism; man again became his own ultimate. Man was the measure of all things and thus his own law and god. As a result, because there no higher law was recognized, the state became totalitarian, and the Renaissance and the twentieth century scientific revolution are the two great periods of totalitarianism in the post-Roman world.

The moral consequences of the Renaissance were relativism and aesthetic individualism. The only law binding man was his own taste. For the Renaissance perspective, "Good and bad are not absolute concepts, but products of their time...Good is what conforms to its time, what corresponds to actual society—in other words, good usage. Bad is what is out of date—the antiquated."[6] The goal of the Renaissance was to strip man of the bondage of law and leave him free to sin as he pleased, subject only to his own taste, to personal aesthetics.

---

[6] John S. White, *Renaissance Cavalier* (New York: Philosophical Library, 1959), 13.

This too is Murphy's goal; it is not so much a particular scientific breakthrough in botany, physics, chemistry, or something else. It is to "free" man from law, God's law, in the name of science, the new area of the gods, or man-gods. The mythology of science is the old myth offered to Eve, "Ye shall be as God, knowing [i.e., determining for yourself] good and evil" (Gen. 3:5).

This new mythology of science is therefore hostile to the old fact of God. Somehow God and His world must be disproved. Somehow too the evolutionary scheme must be proved. Life on other planets is no mere matter of curiosity with these men: it is a religious hope. When reports indicated that "the surface of Venus has temperatures ranging from 675° F. at the equator to 300° F. at the poles," we are told that "Lingering hopes that Venus might support life received a blow."[7] Now this is curious language for supposedly objective science. Supposedly "science" and scientists are interested in the results, not in proving a hope, in getting at the truth of something, not in making a case. The pleasure should have been in getting some kind of knowledge about Venus. But the knowledge was a "blow" to "lingering hopes"! But this is not all. The same issue of *Science Digest* carried the sad report on Mariner 4's photos under the title, "Obituary of a Planet." The unhappy story began, "Mars is dead. Geologically, but not biologically...When the analysis committee saw the clear photos that came in later, they were 'shocked really beyond belief,' and the speculation was confirmed." However, the committee did not entirely give up hope. They stated that "the Mariner photos neither demonstrate nor preclude the possible existence of life on Mars."[8] Mars is geologically dead, but hope for biological life is not surrendered. And recent speculations have revived the hope. Scientific objectivity and impartiality? On the

---

[7.] "The Late Science News," *Science Digest*, vol. 58, no. 4 (October, 1955): 4.

[8.] Bruce H. Frisch, "The Astronomy Story. Obituary of a Planet," in *ibid.*, 8 f.

contrary, this is a passionate dedication by the new magicians to the myths of their own making.

The scientists believe themselves, modestly, to be the new gods of the universe. Alan Smith asks humbly, in one article, "Can we improve on nature too much?" He states that "there is no law, natural or otherwise, that says nature cannot be duplicated through the use of other materials; and without drawing the idea out any further, it's sufficient to say that any good camera lens is optically superior to the eye." Automation and cybernetics are an indication of the possibilities for the future. "It's also well within the bounds of future possibility to build a highly complex machine whenever the situation demands."[9]

The optimism of science is boundless. Having declared that scientists will create a new sun, it is nothing for them to plan the creation of life. A famous biochemist has said, "This century will go down in history as the century when life ceased to be a mystery...Life is only chemistry. It is complicated, yes. But we no longer have any reason to believe it is beyond human understanding."[10] There is, of course, no trace of humility in this statement, but it is absurd for gods to be humble; humility belongs to men. A British scientist has stated, "I feel certain that in another decade or two we ourselves will be able to create life. I no longer find it necessary to believe in God." Of these scientists, Gunther writes with assurance, "They have found the key to life."[11]

This then is the new mythology of man, the mythology of science. It expresses the basic presuppositions of the humanism of the day, so that its absurdities, contradictions, and pretensions have the ring of infallible truth rather than irrational myth. The magicians of every age have been imposing, and their prestige great. Their accomplishments have often been, whether in Egypt, Babylon, or in the modern

---

[9.] Alan Smith, "Can We Improve on Nature Too Much?." in *ibid.*, 88-91.
[10.] Max Gunther, "The Secret of Life," *The Saturday Evening Post*, 3 July 1965, 25.
[11.] *Ibid.*, 28-29.

world, very real. But their foundations are untenable and their future one of collapse as the myth breaks on the rocks of reality.

Chapter Two

The Concept of Evolution as Cultural Myth

A myth is a traditional explanation of life and its origins which so expresses or coincides with the contemporary spirit that its often radical contradictions and absurdities are never apparent, in that they express the basic presuppositions, however untenable, of everyday life and thought. No age has been free from myths, but, while quick to see the absurdities of outworn myths, it cannot see the contradictions in its own. The myth is a cultural expression embodying the basic motives of the people. For example, among the American Indians, agricultural tribes found their religious faith and expressed their basic myths in terms of the heavenly bodies and the aspects of weather, whereas hunting tribes of the western intermountain area had a cycle of myths concerning the wolf and coyote, both hunters like themselves. However, the scope of the myth is deeper; its motives are basic to the science, religion, sociology, and art, among other things, of the culture. The fundamental motive of the modern era is, as Herman Dooyeweerd has pointed out in *Transcendental Problems of Philosophic Thought, A New Critique of Theoretical Thought*, nature and freedom, both requiring total claims radically in contradiction to one another and yet "necessary" and inevitably true to modern man.

The myth of an age infects every area of life, science and religion included. The Reformation principle, as enunciated by John Calvin, that Scripture is its own interpreter, and that alien categories and principles cannot be used in its interpretation, is anti-myth in purpose, but it has not usually been consistently applied, and throughout Christian history most interpretations of the faith of the Bible have been heavily infected by myth. Contemporary Christianity is largely an expression of the same modern myth which we find in science.

What, specifically, is the nature of this myth? As noted previously, Dooyeweerd has seen its presuppositions to be *nature* and *liberty*. Between the two, a fundamental tension and contradiction exists.

> The dialectical character of this humanist motive is clear. "Liberty" and "nature" are opposite motives, which, in their religious roots cannot be reconciled. When all reality is conceived according to the motive of "nature," that is within the cadre of the "image of the world" created by natural science, there remains in all reality no place for "autonomous and free personality."[1]

Both nature and liberty, however, are pressed into the mold of another principle, all scientific and historical evidences to the contrary, the idea of progress.[2] As against the medieval concepts, with their theological finality and controlled progress, the new concept was rooted in nature and basic to man's liberty. Earlier versions of humanism's myth-making approaches to the concept have been described by Carl Becker in *The Heavenly City of the Eighteenth-Century Philosophers*. To this presupposition, Charles Darwin gave substance in his classical formulation of that myth which summed up all the basic presuppositions of the modern spirit, the doctrine of

---

[1.] Herman Dooyeweerd, *Transcendental Problems of Philosophic Thought*, 73.
[2.] See J. B. Bury, *The Idea of Progress, An Inquiry into Its Origin and Growth* (Macmillan, 1932).

evolution. Essential to this concept of progress was its anti-theological nature: it was a revolt from the sovereign and all-sufficient God who by His predestinating will and eternal counsel brought all things to pass. Yet this theological concept was necessary to science; without it, even in more congenial circumstances, science has risen only to wither. With it, despite all opposition, it flourished, championing a concept of unity of law which is basic to science. Valentine Hepp has called attention to the essentially Calvinistic presuppositions of science in *Calvinism and the Philosophy of Nature*. Bernard Shaw saw the issue as one between Calvin's God and Darwin's evolution, and "the world jumped at Darwin."[3] The world did indeed jump at Darwin, and much as the mythologists try to portray science as persecuted by religion at that time, the plain fact is that the churches themselves for the most part eagerly climbed on the bandwagon, happy to be relieved of beliefs they had long since discarded to all practical intent. Darwin, in the concluding words of the penultimate paragraph of *The Origin of Species*, expressed his own confidence in this new "eternal decree" of progress:

> As all the living forms of life are the lineal descendants of those which lived long before the Cambrian epoch, we may feel certain that the ordinary succession by generation has never once been broken, and that no cataclysm has desolated the whole world. Hence we may look with some confidence to a secure future of great length. And as natural selection works solely by and for the good of each being, all corporeal and mental endowments will tend to progress towards perfection.

Here is the "scientific" formulation of Romans 8:28, "For we know that all things work together for good to them that love God, to them who are the called according to His purpose." It gives man *everything* the God of Scripture and Calvin promises, total control moving to perfection, but *without* any infringement of man's freedom and autonomy! Accordingly,

---

[3.] Cited by Arnold Lunn, ed., in intro. of Douglas Dewar, and H. S. Shelton, *Is Evolution Proved?* (London: Hollis and Carter, 1947), 4.

evolution, as the new myth, must and does promise more than the older theological formulations, but without any interference in man's life, without any being superior to or above him, and without any cosmic teleology to bind man to a purpose alien to his own. This evolution must possess the total scope of God's eternal decree with none of His existence, controls, and requirements! Better a world without meaning than a world with God. For the myth, nothing is more unendurable or "demonic" than the god-concept of Calvin. Herbert J. Muller, for example, prefers this concept of a history without any inherent meaning as the means to preserve man's liberty, but Muller, an historian, is one of those who has reacted against one aspect of myth, the ascription of progress and structure to nature, in favor of the preservation at all costs of man's liberty, which is for him the basic myth.[4]

Others, scientists in particular, cling to the myth in its fullest scope. Physicist Joseph Harold Rush, for example, is anxious to avoid any suggestion of teleology or some kind of god as suggested by the bio-chemist Lecomte du Nouy, in *Human Destiny*. God, of course, is not even considered by Rush. But he also rejects chance. "An organism is not 'a fortuitous concourse of atoms.'" There is structure, organization, everywhere in the universe, each area having its "organizing principle" and all working together. The principle "is inherent in the organization of the atoms themselves."[5]

This, however, he refuses to call teleology, nor does he look to God. He believes in single strand evolution, finds reason for it in the left-handed symmetry of molecules, and yet must speak of life as possibly "an accident that almost did not happen" and states that "carbon-life has evolved from a fortuitous set of circumstances."[6] While Rush cannot affirm spontaneous generation (an exploded concept), he can still

---

4. Herbert J. Muller, "Misuses of the Past," *Horizon* vol. I, 4 March 1959, 4 ff.
5. J. H. Rush, *The Dawn of Life* (Garden City, New York: Hanover House, 1957), 140.
6. *Ibid.*, 101, 156-7, 246.

write: "It would be satisfying to find some kind of life on another planet, even lowly forms, to support our basic thesis that life is a spontaneously originating process." He can insist that "the scientist does not expect something to come from nothing,"[7] even as he must maintain that something did come from nothing.

The Westminster Confession (III, i) declared, "Of God's Eternal Decree":

> God from all eternity did by the most wise and holy counsel of His own will freely and unchangeably ordain whatsoever comes to pass: yet so as thereby neither is God the author of sin, nor is violence offered to the will of the creatures, nor is the liberty or contingency of second causes taken away, but rather established.

Evolution must fulfill a like function, providing the total ordination without affecting the liberty or contingency of second causes and without any sentiency or being in itself. The other aspect of the myth, nature having been so well disposed of by Rush, is man, whose freedom has already been safeguarded by his concept of nature. Man will exercise his own eternal decree, beginning with his life and environment. "Control always breeds the need for more control": it is the essence of man's growth out of his natural environment into manhood, and it involves "a course that leaves no choice ultimately between controlling almost everything or abandoning intelligent control entirely." Man will learn to control "life processes," the biology of his own species, and perhaps ultimately, having conquered both space and death, explore the universe endlessly.[8] Thus the two aspects of the myth both find marvelous fulfillment.

We have an ostensible exception to this faith in progress in George Gaylord Simpson, who is willing to rule out the possibility of unbroken progress in the world apart from man.

[7.] *Ibid.*, 213, 63.

[8.] *Ibid.*, 236, 243-8; especially J. H. Rush, "The Next 10,000 Years," *Saturday Review*, vol. XLI, no. 4 (25 January 1958): 11-13, 36.

Indeed, he denies "that evolution *is* progress," while stating that "progress has occurred within it." Man is, however, although not in every respect, still "the pinnacle so far of evolutionary progress." The destiny of man is in his hands, as is the control of progress, so that progress can be either upward or downward. However, man now has a glimpse through science "as to how to ensure this upward movement." The universe apart from man lacked any purpose or plan, was random and yet patterned in every detail and yet random. Out of all this, man emerges with the "unique quality" of being the captain and master of his fate and destiny; "he, for the first time in the history of life, has increasing power to choose his course and to influence his own future evolution. The possibility of choice can be shown to exist."[9] The more the myth changes, the more it remains the same, more firmly fixed in its main outlines.

Basic to all of this is the myth of progress. Evolution is seen as upward only: "evolution does not go backward."[10] It cannot, because the myth requires a one-directional move, and the strong probability that new forms could fall back, or by natural selection be bred out of existence, or the whole process be reversed, is an impossibility to the myth. Robert E. D. Clark has pointed out that evolution was a rebellion against exact science in favor of theory and philosophy.[11] One might further add that evolution sets aside some of the basic premises and conclusions of scientific research and is an *anti-scientific* myth. It is hostile to the second law of thermodynamics, and Rush, one of the more sensitive scientists, is partially aware of this, stating, "a living species embodies a unique accumulation of genetic individuality and adaptive wisdom. It is one more insurrection against the Second Law of Thermodynamics."[12]

---

9. George Gaylord Simpson, *The Meaning of Evolution* (New York: Mentor Books, 1957), 107, 123, 174, 180 f.

10. Rush, *The Dawn of Life*, 63.

11. Robert E. D. Clark, *Darwin, Before and After* (London: Paternoster Press, 1950), 90ff.

12. Rush, *op. cit.*, 240.

Unlimited scope of freedom and autonomy for life is made possible by this inexplicable and truly miraculous "insurrection" which makes man more supernatural than medieval philosophy ever did. Whether it be spontaneous generation or the potentialities seen in neutrons, as witness William J. Pollard, it is clear that if one speaks in terms of chromosomes, neutrons, or the like, *any* miracle is possible in terms of this myth, whereas if one speaks in terms of God, *no* miracle is acceptable to autonomous man.[13]

Occasionally, a scientist is aware of the fact that a myth is the governing principle of science now, as witness the anthropologist Loren C. Eiseley.[14] However, Eiseley also speaks of evolution as a basic and provable fact, dating the emergence of man as "somewhere between about a million and 600,000 years ago, quite suddenly," and gives a vivid account of this great blessed event which "took place in silence."[15] Some, aware of the impossibility of the whole thing, exercise a fertile imagination to create a way out of the impasse, as witness Fred Hoyle's concept of continuous creation, which creates new questions for every one "solved."[16]

For the most part, the myth is accepted as true and needing no proof. Martin Gardiner, because Mortimer J. Adler of the University of Chicago called evolution a "popular myth," included him in his study of quacks and frauds, *Fads and*

[13.] See William G. Pollard, "The Cosmic Drama," *Faculty Paper*, and also the same in *Best Articles and Stories*, vol. III, no. 10 (December 1959). This contrast is especially marked in Pollard, Director of the Atomic Laboratories at Oak Ridge and an Episcopal clergyman, who, while seeing an "Almighty Author" behind the universe, nevertheless reserves the miraculous to neutrons and speaks of the universe having "generated within itself a consciousness capable of responding" to the wonder of "creation and evolution." For him, however, creation is not historical and "not a possible object of scientific inquiry or demonstration," whereas evolution is.

[14.] Loren C. Eiseley, "The Secret of Life," *Harper's Magazine*, October 1953.

[15.] Eiseley, "An Evolutionist Looks at Modern Man," *The Saturday Evening Post*, vol. 230, no. 43, 26 April 1958.

[16.] Fred Hoyle, *The Nature of the Universe* (New York: Harper, 1950). For comments on Hoyle, see Paul A. Zimmerman, ed., *Darwin, Evolution, and Creation* (St. Louis: Concordia, 1959), 85-91. For excellent analyses of various other concepts, see John W. Klotz, *Genes, Genesis, and Evolution* (St. Louis: Concordia, 1955).

Fallacies in the Name of Science: "*The Curious Theories of Modern Pseudo-scientists and the Strange, Amusing, and Alarming Cults that Surround Them. A Study in Human Gullibility.*" To question the myth or to request proof is to be pilloried as a modern heretic and fool. For an example of the kind of "proof" offered, note Alfred Romer's "Darwin and the Fossil Record," in *Natural History*, subtitled by that publication thus: "In the century since Darwin's controversial theory first appeared, paleontologists have established a solid foundation for evolution."[17] This "solid foundation" turns out merely to be more extensive data and the belief that the picture is "in harmony" with evolution rather than special creation. There is no awareness that the harmony, in either instance, could be essentially in the mind of the beholder and in terms of his basic presuppositions. Clyde Kluckhorn, for example, states: "Darwin's contribution was much less the accumulation of new knowledge than the creation of a theory which put in order data already known."[18]

But while the new order ran contrary to scientific knowledge, it fulfilled the requirements of the commanding cultural myth and thereby explained the data as nothing else could. Jacques Barzun, commenting on its success, notes that it placed the opposition in an immediate minority and "superseded all other beliefs." "Nor is it hard to understand why it did, for it fulfilled the basic requirement of any religion by subsuming all phenomena under one cause."[19] The first edition of Darwin's *On the Origin of Species* appeared on November 24, 1859, and all 1,250 copies sold out on the day of publication. It continued to sell at an amazing rate. Its influence in every area of life was rapid and far-reaching.[20]

According to von Uexhull, Darwinism "is more a religion than a science."[21] Its tenacity is precisely that it provides an all-

---

[17.] *Natural History*, vol. LXVII (October 1959): 457.

[18.] Clyde Kluckhorn, *Mirror for Man*, 25.

[19.] Jacques Barzun, *Darwin, Marx, Wagner, Critique of a Heritage* (Boston: Little, Brown, 1941), 73.

[20.] See, for example, Richard Hofstadter, *Social Darwinism in American Thought* (Boston: Beacon Press, 1955).

[21.] Cited by Lunn, *op. cit.*, 6.

inclusive and exclusive worldview, which, wherever Christianity has had any influence, man comes to expect of his working concepts. As such, it exercises a function parallel to orthodox, Biblical Christianity, and with far more respectability, as an "official" and "established church" for the requirements of autonomous man. And, because at present there is nothing to replace it but a return to the hated Father's house, its powers of tenacity and resistance are far greater than its weaknesses would indicate. This unhappy situation is made more difficult by the fact that the Church, always predisposed to accept the contemporary mythologies, is today a particularly devout exponent of and adherent to the myth of the age. Only occasionally do pockets of resistance appear and too seldom is the burden of warring against myth undertaken. At this point, with reference to the doctrine of creation, significant work has been done in this era by Cornelius Van Til in *The Defense of the Faith, The New Modernism,* etc. But, such is the power of myths that, by their side, truth has an incredible sound.

Meanwhile, the myth flourishes. And even as in the Middle Ages the humble and devout believers in the current myths saw and talked with saints and angels, having experiences denied by, or embarrassing to, the doctors of the Church, so the humble and devout believers today have their experiences in terms of the myth. They see abominable snowmen and other creatures who are the "missing link," flying saucers, and space ships, talk to men from other planets, and give us the latest news from space. These experiences are ridiculous to the mythologists of official science, but the underlying premises are theirs.[22] Perhaps the main error of these devout and naive men is that they lack the scope of imagination scientists possess. After all, Kenneth Heuer, a specialist in planetary astronomy and a fellow of Britain's Royal Astronomical Society, believes it possible, when our solar system perishes, and other systems wane as well, that man may construct his

---

[22.] See Kenneth W. Gatland and Kerek D. Dempster, *The Inhabited Universe* (Greenwich, Conn.: Fawcett, 1959).

own sun, operate it by subatomic energy, suspend it in the sky to hold "the hovering demons of cold and darkness at bay," and thus continue his existence as virtual god and creator indefinitely![23] Having such rich promises from his myth, what, after all, is there left for modern man to desire—unless it be the crucified truth? The scientist, we are assured, has no need of the "God-concept" when he has himself; it can add nothing to his inquiry or theory, and the idea of God may be "no more than a shadow of our own ignorance." His ignorance does indeed cast a great and mythological shadow, but its name is not God. And, as man throws more satellites into space and dreams of creating suns, the shadow grow deeper and more terrifying in his own being; he becomes more deeply divided within himself and at odds with life itself. "The hovering demons of cold and darkness" have not been kept at bay from man's inner being.

[23.] Kenneth Heuer, "The End of the World," *Panorama, The Laurel Review*, no. 1 (December 1957): 74- 85. Adapted from Heuer's *The Next Fifty Billion Years*.

Chapter Three

Orwell's 1984:
Horror or Hope?

When George Orwell wrote *1984*, he saw, from the vantage of 1948, a new world already in process of development around him and implicit in all the presuppositions which governed his day. For Orwell, *1984* is 1948 more openly revealed. That Orwell viewed this scientific socialist future with horror is well known and obvious; that *1984* became a symbol of a monstrous and dehumanized world is equally obvious. It comes as a surprise to many that the term "1984" is often used as a symbol of a *glorious* future despite full awareness of the meaning of Orwell's work. Thus, a major periodical cites 1984 as the symbolic date when man has overcome death.[1] More importantly, the *New Scientist* carried a series of articles on 1984, published in two volumes as *The World in 1984*.[2] These articles give almost unanimously, with a professor of poetry markedly dissenting, a glowing picture of 1984.[3] Why should "1984," *the ultimate horror* for Orwell,

---

[1.] Frederick Pohl, "Intimations of Immortality," in *Playboy*, vol. 11, no. 6, June 1964, 79 f., 160-167.

[2.] Negil Calder, ed., *The World in 1984* (Baltimore: Penguin Books, 1965).

[3.] The dissent came from Sir Herbert Read, "Atrophied Muscles and Empty Art," in *The World in 1984*, vol. 2, 88-92. Read saw science triumphant in 1984, poetry "totally" gone; "composers like Beethoven, Wagner, and Stravinsky will be forgotten." It will be a world of entertainment instead of meaning: "It will be a gay world. There will be lights everywhere except in the mind of man, and the fall of the last civilization will not be heard above the incessant din."

represent the beginning of ultimate bliss for so many
scientists? Why should they even invite comparison to
Orwell's vision by using 1984 as their symbolic date? The
answer is that for them Orwell's disenchantment with the
brave new world of science revealed strong elements of
"utopianism" in his thinking. Orwell did not renounce
socialism: he only feared what he believed in. Van Riessen has
rightly observed that:

> What is tragic in Orwell is that he does not himself know
> what to defend in opposition to this tyranny. He has
> nothing with which to oppose it as he lacks a position of
> his own. In this he is like the Party. His conception is that
> of a negative freedom, a freedom from tyranny,
> culminating in a sensual, norm-less love for Julia. *Orwell*
> can oppose a nihilism of freedom, the nihilism of *Sartre*.
> Therefore he cannot "stand firm" in his freedom (Gala-
> tians 5:1). His freedom is based on his own power, existing
> solely because of himself, and, consequently, readily
> destroyed when his own life is at stake.[4]

Orwell did not hold to Christian ethics; he could only
briefly oppose amoral freedom to amoral power. His
"utopianism" was his failure to overcome an ethical
repugnance to amoral power: he judged 1984 by a Christian
ethical horror he could not believe in. For the scientists who
visualized a glorious era in 1984, the only admissible ethics
were pragmatic. According to one social scientist, who believes
that science can save us,

> Ethical norms will change in the future as they have in the
> past, and human institutions, including the church, will
> accommodate themselves to change in the future as in the
> past. A developed social science will greatly facilitate this
> adjustment, because through science man can secure a very
> much more adequate knowledge of the consequences of
> different types of conduct, instead of relying upon ancient
> and arbitrary authority for this counsel.[5]

[4.] H. Van Riessen (Donald High Freeman, translator), *The Society of the Future* (Philadelphia: Presbyterian and Reformed Publishing Company,
1957), 66.
[5.] George A. Lundberg, *Can Science Save Us?* (New York: Longmans,
Green, 1961), 109.

The implication is clear: there are no absolute ethics. Nothing is right or wrong in any ultimate sense, but only in a practical sense, in terms of "consequences," to use Lundberg's criterion. Orwell's horror was unscientific, because if there is no absolute truth, there is no absolute evil. As a result, "1984" is an attractive concept to such scientists, because it provides greater scope for scientific experimentation and planning.

The premises of such thinking are evolutionary. The evolutionary concept presupposes and requires several important ideas and conclusions. First of all, God is either bypassed or denied. For all forms of evolutionary thinking God is irrelevant. If He exists, He has nothing essential to do with a world which has evolved out of its own inner forces and thus is a law unto itself. The God-hypothesis is thus only retained by persons who are trying to maintain a formal but nonessential relationship between Christianity and evolution. For the consistent evolutionist, the energy inherent in the material universe is seen as sufficient cause for the development and proliferation of life and being. The God-hypothesis is irrelevant. Man's need for it is psychological, since he does not yet control all aspects of life; when he establishes that control, he will discard such a belief, and "Belief is simply an emotional identification with a concept and as such is not open to question or challenge."[6]

> The recognition that Man's brain has, apparently, unlimited capabilities and that the horizons of human culture cannot yet be perceived is not to deny his need for a belief in some super-organic being. Until we have established direct control over all aspects of life and have come to accept the inevitability of organic death, we apparently must turn, as have all men in the past, to some concept of divine supremacy.[7]

When man has "established direct control over all aspects of life," *then* this psychological necessity for "some concept of

---

[6] Bertram S. Kraus, *The Basis of Human Evolution* (New York: Harper and Row, 1964), 359.
[7] *Ibid.*, 360.

divine supremacy," decided by "each individual...according to his emotional and intellectual requirements,"[8] will disappear, for man will be his own god, his own source of total control. Meanwhile, God is only psychologically and not meta-physically real to man; He exists as a need, not as God.

Second, because there is no God, there is no ultimately true law, no absolute concept of right and wrong. No God means no law, and no law means that nothing is a crime, and hence all acts are equally valid in terms of morality, although perhaps not equally practical or workable. In this sense, honesty can be the best policy if it works best, but dishonesty can also be the best policy wherever it works better than honesty.

Third, by dropping the God-concept, the idea of good and evil as ultimate moral concepts is also dropped. Nothing is good or evil of itself, and the very terms "good" and "evil" reflect an older, "obsolete" world of absolutes, of God's truth and law. Good and truth are whatever works, whatever serves man's purposes. Man is not *under* law but *over* law; therefore, man cannot be judged as good or evil, but man judges things to be good or evil, useful or useless, as they serve him. Scientific, humanistic man is *beyond good and evil.* Good and evil are alike mythological concepts; thus man cannot be evil. Therefore, the world-planners of "1984" cannot do evil, because evil does not exist: there are merely successful experiments in human engineering and unsuccessful ones.

Fourth, as is now clear, because God is a myth, the evolutionary and empirical approach to man's problems must be "scientific," i.e., experimental, and man is thus the prime laboratory test animal. Experimentation with man is already in process. The "biological revolution" claims that it soon can alter man's heredity as well as transplant organs.[9] The mind of

---

8. *Ibid.*

9. See "Control of Life," *Life* Magazine, vol. 59, no. 11, 10 September 1965; no. 12, 17 September 1965; no. 13, 24 September 1965; no. 14, 1 October 1965; Fred Warshofsky, *The Rebuilt Man: The Story of Spare-Parts Surgery* (New York: Thomas Y. Crowell, 1965). See also Harold M. Schmeck, Jr., *The Semi-Artificial Man, A Dawning Revolution in Medicine* (New York: Walker and Company, 1965).

man is to be controlled by psychiatry through chemistry and electronics.[10] Man's health is being socially treated by the fluoridation of water, and now "contraceptivating" the water to effect birth control, and then allowing women to conceive by taking a "neutralizing agent" to offset the effect of the water, has been seriously proposed.[11] Another scientist has proposed deep-freezing the dying and rejuvenating them at a later date when their particular ailment has been overcome; man can in this way be kept alive until immortality is achieved. Until then, we shall have what he terms "the Freezer-Centered Society."[12] The list can be greatly extended. It is sufficient to note that *man* is now the prime guinea pig of the scientific planners.

Fifth, every experiment, to be valid, requires total control of all factors. Hence, the scientific society must be fully totalitarian, otherwise it will not work, nor will it be scientific. Science, according to Titiev, proceeds on the "faith" that "all phenomena that are presently unknown to humans will some day be brought into the sphere of the known, and that when this happens more and more things will be made subject to the law of controlled causation."[13] The "law of controlled causation" is basic to science:

> Simple knowledge of cause and effect relationships may not in itself lead to greater reliance on science than on supernaturalism. What is much more likely to prove effective is based on *the law of controlled causation.* Whenever men are able to demonstrate that they can produce stated effects by manipulating their causes, the

---

[10.] Robert Coughlan, "Control of the Brain, Part I, Behavior by Electronics," in *Life*, vol. 54, no. 10, 8 March 1963, 90-106; Robert Coughlan, "Control of the Brain, Part II, The Chemical Mind-Changers," in *Life*, vol. 54, no. 11, 15 March 1963, 81-94.

[11.] *Canadian Intelligence Service*, 3, "'Contraceptivated' Water," vol. 15, no. 10, October 1965, quoting an article by Sidney Katz in the Toronto *Star*, 8 October 1965, based on a report by Dr. Joseph W. Goldzieher in *Pacific Medicine and Surgery*.

[12.] Robert C. W. Ettinger, *The Prospect of Immortality* (Garden City, New York: Doubleday, 1964).

[13.] Mischa Titiev, M., *Introduction to Cultural Anthropology* (New York: Henry Holt, 1959), 348.

phenomena with which they deal move from the realm of religion to the realm of science. Thus, as more facts become scientifically known, the law of controlled causation covers ever more cases, then man's *reliance* on the supernatural shrinks. This is merely another way of saying that as the amount of knowledge in a society goes up, there is a proportionate decrease of its dependence on supernaturalism. To test the validity of this hypothesis one has only to note that genuine *reliance* on the supernatural remains strongest in sophisticated societies in precisely those areas, like death, where the law of controlled causation cannot be said to operate.[14]

In terms of this evolutionary perspective, science is not so much the *understanding* of things as the *controlling* of things. The government and providence of God are replaced by the government and providence of man, and the divine predestination gives way to predestination by scientific planners. A Christian society, by leaving predestination to God, leaves man in liberty and denies the right of independent control to any human agency; all human powers and authorities are carefully governed and circumscribed by the Word of God. A scientific society, in order to be scientific, must bring all things under the strict control of scientists so that, by means of the law of controlled causation, the desired results can be socially and individually attained.

By means of science, man's needs are to be realized. In terms of evolutionary science, man's needs are humanistic. According to Alexander Robertus Todd, Professor of Organic Chemistry at the University of Cambridge, a life peer and Nobel Prize recipient for Chemistry in 1957, the goals of mankind are "freedom from hunger and want, adequate warmth and protection, and freedom from disease."[15] The scientist, by his ability to effect desired results through scientific controls, is best able to give man what man seeks. Moreover, Isidor Isaac Rabi, Associate Director of the

---

[14.] *Ibid.*, 346.
[15.] Professor Lord Todd, "Science and Human Goals. A British View: Working With What We Know," *The World in 1984*, vol. I, 9.

Radiation Laboratory of the Massachusetts Institute of Technology, Chairman of the general advisory committee to the Atomic Energy Commission, Higgins Professor of Physics at Columbia University, member of the President's Science Advisory Committee, and Nobel Prize recipient for Physics in 1944, assures us with all the wisdom of his position that, "Somehow the scientific education diminishes the ambition for power and worldly influence."[16] Rabi thus believes that we can trust the scientists to be disinterestedly concerned with man's destinies because of "a feeling for the possibilities of development or evolution in a current situation" and "a certain sense of rightness and equity, sometimes naive but rarely on the wrong track."[17] Joshua Lederberg observed that after aeons of evolution "by random chemistry," "our culture is achieving knowledge and control of its biological instruments that are capable of purposefully altering them."[18] Lederberg made some predictions about areas of control which he believed were soon to come:

(1) The successful transplantation of vital organs: heart, liver, limbs. The technical barriers will be overcome long before we can reach a moral consensus on the organization of the market for allocation of precious parts.

(2) Artificial prosthetic organs. Unfortunately not yet being developed with the necessary vigour to overtake the preceding.

(3) In consequence of these, and probably other advances in, say, protein biochemistry, a sudden increase in the expectation, or prolongability, of life. With a wider range of technical resources will come a corresponding expansion of the scale of the useful cost of maintaining a given personality. Whatever our humanitarian predilections, discrepancies in the availability of these resources must widen.

[16.] I. I. Rabi, "Science and Human Values. An American View: The Scientist in Public Affairs," *ibid.*, 14.

[17.] *Ibid.*

[18.] Joshua Lederberg, "Fundamental Science. A Crisis in Evolution," *ibid.*, 25. Lederberg is Professor of Genetics and Director of the J. P. Kennedy, Jr. Laboratories for Molecular Medicine at Stanford.

(4) More optimistically, the modification of the developing human brain through treatment of the foetus or infant. At least some modifications (like those used primitively now in the control of metabolic diseases) can be expected to be constructively applied to "normal" children, and might well exceed the present bounds of genetic and developmental variations.

(5) 'Clonal' reproduction, through nuclear transplantation. The prototype for this suggestion is the transplantation of a nucleus from an adult tissue back into an amphibian egg from which the natural nucleus has been removed with (sometimes) normal development of this egg. It should be recalled that vegetative reproduction, occasionally concealed under outward trappings of sexuality, is an important feature of the plant world, and a few primitive animals. The experiment has yet to be attempted in a mammal. Apart from its place in the narcissistic perpetuation of a given genotype, the technique would have an enormous impact on predetermination of sex; on the avoidance of hereditary abnormalities, as well as positive genetics; on cultural acceleration through education within a clone; and on more far-reaching experiments on the reconstitution of the human genotype.[19]

Lederberg's predictions are commonplace among scientists today. Thus, the biologist, Dr. James Bonner, of the California Institute of Technology, at a meeting of the Pacific Division of the Association for the Advancement of Science, made even more far-reaching statements:

New discoveries on controlling living cells are leading to staggering possibilities. You soon can grow a new heart, or four hands, or bigger brain. A synthetic man is a distinct possibility....

...Bonner was summing up his latest research with living cells, research that made him further predict in an interview:

[19] *Ibid.*, 26 f.

1. New organs—heart, lungs, arms, legs—not transplants, but new tissue grown by each individual as the need arises after disease or accident.

2. Bigger brains with better learning capacity—vital, he believes, if men are not to be made obsolete by computers.

Bonner says the growth of new organs will be possible "in less than a generation."

"My son will be able to have four hands—and he might need them to keep up with the pace of our changing world," Bonner says. He adds wistfully: "But it probably won't come in my time."

Bonner is 54: his son James is 15.

Growth of bigger brains, he believes, is "somewhat further away—we don't know as much about the brain as we do the body—but it is coming."

"We are not far from the time when we can take a cell—any cell—and tell it to become an embryo, or heart tissue, or bone, or something else.

"We are learning how to turn on the genes in the nucleus which tell a cell to become one thing and to turn off the genes which tell it to become something else."[20]

Not only will man be the object of scientific control and development, but nature also will be controlled. Francois Bourliere believes that "1984" will mean the end of "untamed Nature," for "the world of 1984 will certainly leave but little place for wild animals." "Herbicides and insecticides will lead to a total monopoly of Man on plant and animal productivity." All productive areas will be used for scientific farming and competing life will be killed by herbicides and insecticides. "All wild life will in such activities certainly be considered as competitive with man and therefore destined to extermination." Only "a few natural preserves" will be

---

20. Ralph Dighton, "Genetic Experts Predict Spare-Parts for Humans," Santa Ana, California, *Register*, 4 October 1965, A13. See also G. H. Beale, "Changing Cell Heredity," *The World in 1984*, vol. 1, 199 ff.

retained "for scientific or aesthetic reasons."[21] The use of herbicides and scientific farming are seen as basic to scientific agriculture by Sir William Slater and Professor Koichi Yamada.[22] Weather will be controlled, and hurricanes will disappear. The California coast will have a new climate with an established temperature. The state will construct "offshore islands and bars, breakwaters, lagoons, and small curving bays." The length of the shoreline is to be tripled.[23]

Foods also will be products of science, although not as early as 1984:

> Of course it is conceivable that by 1984 we shall produce our food in factories, without animals or plants, exploiting the most far-reaching biological discovery of the last few years, the synthesis of proteins in cell-free systems. Eventually we should be able to manufacture satisfactory foodstuffs in great chemical plants, where masses of ribosomes would be supplied with synthetic amino-acids and long-lived messenger RNAs, with energy-yielding phosphates produced by irradiating chloroplasts with laser-tuned light of the most effective wavelength. But that technological dream is nearer fifty than twenty years ahead, unless resources are put into these lines of research at something like the level that was used to develop the atom bomb. In 1984 we will probably still be depending on more or less conventional agriculture.[24]

Other possibilities cited are environmental control, snow "melted before it sticks to the ground," and "an air-

---

[21.] Francois Bourliere, "Natural Resources. A New Balance Between Man and Nature," in *The World in 1984*, vol. 1, 53 f. Bourliere is Professor of Gerontology of the Faculty of Medicine at Paris University. Ironically, he is President of the International Union for the Conservation of Nature and Natural Resources.

[22.] *Ibid.*, 64, 133.

[23.] Roger Revelle, "Oceans. A Long View From the Beach," *ibid.*, 106 ff. Revelle is Director, Scripps Institution, University of California.

[24.] C. H. Waddington, "Human Mind. Science and Wisdom," *ibid.*, vol. 2, 13. Waddington is Buchanan Professor of Genetics, University of Edinburgh, and President of the International Union of Biological Sciences.

conditioning shed...erected over the entire community," the mountains built "on a former flat plain" by bull-dozers.[25]

In this brave new world, scientists will of course be the peacemakers. Scientists will also "have achieved their major goal, the drafting and general acceptance of a new system of education, based on the ideals of fundamental common interests of the human species, and on the development of a sense of belonging to mankind as a whole." The result of this education will be world government. "Thus, by the end of this century, when the generation brought up in this new spirit will take over, the establishment of a World Authority...will follow as a matter of course."[26]

Crime will also be taken care of by the scientists. We are told that "In any increasingly competitive society...we must expect rising figures of crime." Moreover, not only a competitive society, but also a Christian one perpetuates crime. "The risk of criminality will be enhanced, too, if the present association between moral teaching and the Christian religion is perpetuated."[27] Morality must be, we are warned, disassociated from the supernatural to avoid a moral breakdown.

> Indeed our present failure, in a scientific age, to dissociate morality from remarkably improbable dogmas must be counted as one of the most vulnerable features of contemporary society. If the next twenty years does not see general recognition of a purely secular morality, we must not be surprised to find that moral standards have been emptied away along with the Christian bath-water.[28]

[25.] Martin Meyerson and Margy Meyerson, "Cities. Multiple Choices," *ibid.* Martin Meyerson is Professor of Urban Development, University of California, and Margy Ellin Meyerson, his wife, is a former Research Director of the American Society of Planning Officials.

[26.] Joseph Rotblat, "International Relations. Scientists as Peacemakers," *ibid.*, vol. 2, 121. Rotblat was "a member of the British team at Los Alamos during the development of the atomic bomb" and is now Professor of Physics at the University of London.

[27.] Barbara Wootton, "Britain, Winner and Losers in the Rat Race," *ibid.*, vol. 2, 133. Barbara Frances Wootton is Professor of Social Studies at the University of London and a life-peeress since 1958.

[28.] *Ibid.*, vol. 2, 134.

What kind of morality did Wootton have in mind? First of all, the social scientist would replace the traditional law court and transform it "into social agencies for the prevention of crime."[29] Morality is thus in essence the scientific totalitarian state. In the area of sexuality, the new morality (or old sin) would, and indeed does prevail:

> By 1984, the practice of adult homosexuality will surely have ceased to be criminal, and only the deeply religious will be shocked by pre-marital unchastity. Concern for a child's welfare will have finally swamped considerations of its parents' marital state, and divorce by consent (after how many years of marriage?) will be attainable legally, not, as now, only by subterfuge and perjury. Conceivably also, the sane and humane values of the many intelligent young people who have shown that they prefer Alderson-marching to rat-racing will have had a more profound influence upon our whole way of life than some of their faint-hearted elders can yet envisage.[30]

Man's economic outlook would no longer be "the forms of an ancient economy of scarcity which was his heritage for five millennia," but rather the sense of his own capacity to create and remake the world.[31]

This confidence concerning the future is commonplace in scientific literature. Colonization of the universe is seriously discussed.[32] Shock and sadness are expressed that Venus and Mars apparently do not support life.[33] Ronald N. Bracewell, director of Stanford's Radio Astronomy Institute, believes that "intelligent beings may be transmitting radio messages between the planets in outer space...but, unfortunately, 'we aren't tuned in.'"[34] We are also assured that, in the age of

---

29. *Ibid.*

30. *Ibid.*, vol. 2, 135.

31. L. V. Berkner, "North America, The Rise of the Metropolis," *ibid.*, vol. 2, 147. Berkner is president of the Graduate Research Center of the Southwest, Dallas, Texas.

32. Fritz Leiber, "Homes for Men in the Stars," *Science Digest*, vol. 58, no. 3 (September 1965): 53-57.

33. "Sizzling Venus," *Science Digest*, vol. 58, no. 4 (October 1965): 4; Bruce H. Frisch, "Obituary of a Planet," *ibid.*, 8 f

34. "Are Space Beings Sending Messages?" San Francisco *News-Call-Bulletin*, 28 February 1963, 1.

automation and bionics, "the science of systems which function, after the manner of or in a manner characteristic of or resembling, living systems,"..."a machine might grow replacement parts to alter its own circuitry."

> It's also within the bounds of future possibility to build a highly complex machine that is quite capable of building (reproducing) similar machines whenever the situation demands.[35]

But this is not all. Even more amazing things are planned for man and are the subjects of recent experimentation:

> Transplanting of memory from one brain to another by injection was disclosed yesterday by a group of psychologists at the University of California at Los Angeles.
>
> The experiment was made with rats but Dr. Allan L. Jacobson said "We can certainly imagine that benefits might result for humans in the long run."
>
> Jacobson, assistant professor of psychology, said the transplanted substance was ribonucleic acid (RNA), long suspected to be involved in the memory process.
>
> The RNA molecule is similar to that of deoxyribonucleic acid (DNA), the molecule that carries hereditary blueprints from one generation to the next. Current theory is that RNA may encode memory much as DNA encodes genetic information.
>
> Jacobson and his associates trained rats to go to a food when a certain click was sounded. They extracted RNA from the brains of the trained rats and injected it into the bodies of untrained rats. The injected rats showed a "significant tendency"—7 out of 25—to go to the cup when a click sounded, without previous training, Jacobson said. A control group of uninjected rats responded in this manner only one time in 25, he said....[36]

[35.] Alan Smith, "Can We Improve on Nature Too Much?," *Science Digest* (October, 1965): 90.

[36.] Ralph Dighton, "Transplanting Memory by Injection May Be Next," Oakland (California) *Tribune*, 6 August 196, 1.

The president of the American Chemical Society, Dr. Charles C. Price, "has proposed making the artificial creation of life a national goal—one that could be achieved in 20 years."[37]

But this is not all. A British astronomer has speculated on what man can do when the universe begins to die:

> If modern theories of creation are correct, the main body of stars was formed at the same time; and when the sun is dying, the entire universe will be filled with dead or dying stars. It is believed, however, that the process of star formation is still in progress so that there may be some live stars with planets to colonize when this cosmic catastrophe takes place.
>
> Still another possibility would be to construct our own sun, a source of heat and light which might be suspended in the sky and hold the hovering demons of cold and darkness at bay. This artificial sun would operate by subatomic energy. In the remaining years of grace, man might learn how to run the carbon cycle. Hydrogen, the fuel, is abundant, and other light atoms, such a lithium, are also plentiful sources of energy. With several billions of years of time at his disposal for research, man should be able to develop cheap, abundant, and manageable subatomic power.[38]

Against this boundless scientific optimism, a few scientific voices are raised. Professor Zenon Bacq, Professor of Physiopathology and Radiobiology in the University of Liege, Belgium, raises the question, "What is going to happen when the natural equilibrium between man and viruses is disturbed?"[39] "Temporary sterilization of men," he states, is contemplated, and "Sterilizing substances are already present in chickens and beef offered for human consumption. Misfortunes of two kinds may be predicted: somatic troubles

---

37. "'National Goal.' A Plan for U.S.—Create Life in 20 Years," San Francisco *Chronicle*, 14 September 1965, 1, "Birth in a Test Tube Proposed as Newest U.S. 'National Goal.'"

38. Kenneth Heuer, "The End of the World," *Panorama, The Laurel Review*, no. 1 (December 1957): 82f.

39. Z. M. Bacq, "Health. A Vicious Circle of Chemicals?" *The World in 1984*, vol. 2, 25.

affecting only the individual and genetic troubles affecting the species."[40] Moreover,

> The development of the so-called diseases of civilization seems unavoidable. It will lead not only to endless troubles for medical men in research and practice, but also to psychological and legal complications. Let us take just one case. The control by drugs of reproduction and sexual activity is spreading, because it is needed in order to limit the accelerated growth of the human population on the Earth. Beyond the estimated number of six billion for the year 2000, great troubles must be expected. For the sake of more food, the use of insecticides, fungicides, and artificial fertilizers is going to spread and intensify itself in all countries, with the consequence that concentrations of these substances in the water and food may increase up to the danger point. The great luxuries will be pure water from a spring, plants and animals carefully raised by the consumer himself in the absence of chemical contamination, fish caught in the high seas away from the coast. Thanks to increasing leisure, men (at least the most active of them) will feel the necessity to become agricultural workers again.[41]

In confirmation of Bacq's fears, recent studies indicate the contamination of the air of the entire world and of rainfall:

> *Insecticides in Air.* British scientists have found traces of various insecticides including DDT and dieldrin in rainwater, implying that the atmosphere is now contaminated by them. Air-borne insecticides may account for the recent discovery of DDT in the fat and liver of Antarctic seals and penguins. One British scientific committee described the situation as "somewhat terrifying."[42]

It is interesting to note the comment of the editor of *New Scientist* in response to Bacq's doubts. Zenon Bacq, we are told, "is sixty."[43] The poor man is apparently too old to have any vision.

---

[40] *Ibid.*, 27.
[41] *Ibid.*, 26.
[42] *Science Digest* (October 1965), 4.
[43] *The World in 1984*, vol. 2, 199.

It is not that scientists are unaware of the dangers. Asimov has noted:

> Already the United States has stored millions of gallons of radioactive liquid underground. Both the United States and Great Britain have dumped concrete containers of fission products at sea. There have been proposals to drop the radioactive wastes in ocean abysses, to store them in old salt mines, to incarcerate them in molten glass and bury the solidified material. But there is always the nervous thought that in one way or another the radioactivity will escape in time and contaminate the soil or the seas. One particularly haunting nightmare is the possibility that a nuclear-powered ship might be wrecked and spill its accumulated fission products into the ocean.[44]

No one, however, is sufficiently alarmed to call a halt to this increasing contamination of air, earth, and water. The general confidence is, that, when a crisis arises, science will come up with an answer. Meanwhile, more important tasks await, such as the Mars project, an attempt to demonstrate the evolutionary process by an exploration of Mars. The official purposes of this project are to:

1. Detect life.
2. Characterize the life forms detected.
3. Determine if such life has a common origin with life on Earth. (This includes both the intertransfer of life between Earth and Mars and a common chemical evolution.)
4. Establish the evolutionary pathway of Martian life.
5. Determine the interaction of life forms with the environment.
6. Look for fossil life and if only fossils are found, determine the factors associated with the extinction of life.
7. If life is not found, discover the factors which prevented its development.[45]

[44.] Isaac Asimov, *The Intelligent Man's Guide to Science*, vol. 1 (New York: Basic Books, 1961), 375.

[45.] Quoted from the *3rd Monthly Progress Report* of Philco, April, 1965, by *Episcopalians for Christ*, vol. IV, nos. vi-ix, Summer 1965, 2 f.

Earlier, Lundberg's belief that science can save us was noted and examined. Knight's summary of Lundberg's faith is of interest:

> In summary, Lundberg's scientism reduced logically to the following proposition: (1) ends, motives, etc., are *data* merely; they present no problem for social science, hence no problem at all; (2) scientific knowledge alone is required for the prediction and control of social events; and (3) the prediction and control of social events is all that is required for the solution of practical social problems (at least to the extent that this is possible). And we should add that, when all this is made generally known by a proper scientific education, men will be content with what is possible so that, in the crucial sense, the social problem will be solved by the application of scientific method.[46]

We saw earlier that the basic syllogism of the evolutionary position is simply this: no God means no law; no law means no crime; no crime means that anything goes. For the ordinary man, this means a license to sexuality of every variety he chooses. For the scientific planners, this means that *man* is the new god of being. The attributes of God, *sovereignty, prediction, and control,* are all claimed by Lundberg for the scientific, and especially the social scientist. The necessary premise of any true theology is simply this: *"With God all things are possible"* (Matt. 19:26). It follows, therefore, that if man be the new god of being, *then with man all things are possible,* i.e., with the scientific planning man. This assurance of unlimited possibilities is basic to the perspective of evolutionary science. There is no humility, because it is unnecessary for a god to be humble. The Biblical God is rendered an unnecessary and useless hypothesis, it is believed, since the scientist progressively predicts and controls events, and, through the law of controlled causation, reduces to nothingness those areas of life over which man has no control.

This control and prediction, however, will not be the property of all men, but of the scientific managers who will

---

46. Frank H. Knight, *On the History and Method of Economics* (University of Chicago Press, Phoenix Books, 1963), 235.

reeducate and remake man, and even create life itself. Men will
have a very near and highly experiment-prone god perpetually
breathing down their necks, with no supernatural God as their
supreme court and ground of liberty. Men are being steadily
educated into this slavery by evolutionary science. Let us note
what an editor has said of education:

> Education is currently very widely held to be the Great
> Panacea for all ills. Whether the problem be social,
> economic, international, or physical—Education, we are
> told, is all that's needed. The trouble with the backward
> nations is that they, unfortunately, didn't have the
> Educational Opportunities the Western nations did. The
> Juvenile Delinquent and the Under privileged People alike
> are what they are for lack of education....
>
> Education is, simply, Slavery...
>
> ...the essence of slavery is the loss of freedom of choice—
> being compelled to learn a new way of life.
>
> The essence of education-the-process is teaching the pupil
> a new way of life, a new set of values and goals, a set of
> ideas which he did not choose to have before....
>
> "We've got to teach them a lesson," has usually meant the
> intention of applying force and pain to change the value-
> judgments of an opposing group. Education, in other
> words....
>
> Now in the language, "to be taught" is a passive verb,
> while "to teach" is active....
>
> Briefly, Education may be a Panacea—but the process of
> applying it does, in actuality, involve enslaving the pupils.
> That's why war has, down through the ages, led to so
> much intellectual and social progress—it's highly
> educational....
>
> The panaceas men have sought for curing the problems of
> inter-human conflicts, down through the ages have all
> been forms of Education "teaching 'em a lesson" or simply
> direct enslavement....

Sure, Education *is* slavery—but that just represents the fact that nothing, not even slavery, is inherently evil or destructive.[47]

We can agree that education *apart from God* is enslavement, because then education refuses to keep its appointed place and seeks to re-make man in the image of his planned society. Christian education must respect the image of God in man and can only seek to conform the student to the requirements of the new man, Jesus Christ, who is "the true Light, which lighteth every man that cometh into the world" (John 1:9).

Man seeks in *1984* this world of total controls, when the scientific planner becomes the new god of a new world. The world of *1984*, however, is the old world of Satan, of the fall of man, of the temptation to "be as gods, knowing good and evil" (Gen. 3:5). It is the old world of the tower of Babel, perpetually doomed to confusion, destruction, and scattering. It is the world of Babylon the Great of *Revelation*, the pretension of man to create a paradise apart from God. It is no brave new world, but instead the age-old doomed world of covenant-breaking man. This new tower of Babel, in process of construction, seems terrifying and imposing, but its collapse and disintegration will be even more awesome and impressive, for "He that sitteth in the heavens shall laugh: the Lord shall have them in derision" (Psalm 2:4). The world of the future shall be God's world, and man in that world shall be only what the predestinating power and control of God intend him to be, for "Known unto God are all his works, from the beginning of the world" (Acts 15:18).

[47.] John W. Campbell, "Panacea," *Analog*, vol. LXXV, no. 6 (August 1965): 5-7, 159.

Chapter Four

The Control of Life

On September 10, 1965, *Life* magazine began a series of articles on the "Control of Life," continued through September 17 and 24, and concluded on October 1. The articles proclaimed an ostensible "biological revolution," and the cover of the first issue announced that "audacious experiments promise decades of added life, super-babies with improved minds and bodies, and even a kind of immortality." The goal of this "biological revolution" is the scientific predestination of man. Scientists are clearly predestinarians today, but it is not predestination by God which they affirm, but predestination by the scientific social engineers. These men can, they believe, very soon "foreordain" their children's intellect and physical characteristics "and of all the generations that follow." The aim of present experimentation is "nothing less than the control of life."[1] According to Dr. Kermit E. Krantz, by control of the fetal development, "maybe we can turn mediocrities into Einsteins.[2]

The articles themselves are meager reading, almost entirely limited to picture captions and accompanying notes. They

[1.] *Life*, vol. 59, no. 11, 10 September 1965, 59, cf. 79.
[2.] *Ibid.*, 67.

read like a press-agent's ballyhoo and could be easily dismissed as hyperbole, except that the experiments cited are at times more audacious than the writer's imagination. One caption reads, "Plant experiments stir speculation that man might reproduce while bypassing sex."[3] Artificial insemination of animals is described, transplants of the embryo to uteruses of other kinds of animals, then the further transplanting into a herd of the original animals.

Dr. E. S. E. Hafez "sees no reason why his techniques could not be applied to people."[4] For future space travel, we are told that planets can be colonized by a competent biologist with test-tube embryos of "people, cows, pigs, chickens, horses— anything we wanted."[5]

The marvels of the new biological revolution are glowingly described: "A man without kidneys gets one in transplant. Gift of life from the dead."[6]

In the description of the transplant of animal organs to humans, and the organs of one man to another, we are reminded that, while success is in the offing, the problem of "tissue rejection" has yet to be overcome to make the experiments successful.[7]

This problem the scientists expect to overcome fairly soon. "An era of rebuilt people" by means of "man-made and transplanted organs" is already visualized.[8] This assurance is so great, that the concluding section, written by Albert Rosenfeld, is titled, "The New Man. What Will He Be Like?." We are asked, "Will man direct his own evolution?" The creation of life as a national goal has been urged by Dr. Charles C. Price, president of the American Chemical Society.

By breaking and controlling the genetic code, man will be able to remake man.

---

3. *Ibid.*, 72.
4. *Ibid*, 75.
5. *Ibid.*, 76.
6. *Life*, vol. 59, no. 12, 17 September 1965, 78.
7. *Ibid.*, 88.
8. *Life*, vol. 59, no. 13, 24 September, 1965, 66 ff.

When that time comes, man's powers will be truly godlike. He may bring into being creatures never before seen or imagined in the universe. He may even choose to create new forms of humanity—beings that might be better adapted to survive on the surface of Jupiter, or on the bottom of the Atlantic Ocean.[9]

Rosenfeld is so sure that this time shall come that he devotes his major attention to the moral issues which this "biological revolution" will raise: "Which men will we assign to play God?"

No one would argue that man couldn't stand some improvement, but having the actual power to do so presents some sticky choices. Who is it that we will appoint to play God for us? Which scientist, which statesman, artist, judge, poet, theologian, philosopher, educator—of which nation, race or creed—will you trust to write the specifications, to decide which characteristics are desirable and which not?[10]

The scientists are already playing God. Dr. Hafez's "egg-implantation techniques" will soon be applied to the human ova by Dr. James L. Burks of the University of Chicago.[11] We are entering an era, Rosenfeld assures us, "when virgin births may become relatively common." Will the family survive the biological revolution, Rosenfeld asks; "Do we want it to survive?," and if so, how? And "what will we substitute for it?" Will marriage survive, and traditional morality?[12] We are reminded that Professor Robert C. W. Ettinger, a physicist, sees quick-freezing of bodies and later rejuvenation and revivification as a coming reality. So sure is Rosenfeld that this "biological revolution" is upon us, that he regards the basic issue to be the preparation of men's minds and thinking to receive this new world of "Scientific Humanism" or "Evolutionary Humanism":

---

9. *Life*, vol. 59, no. 14, 1 October 1965, 100.
10. *Ibid.*
11. *Ibid.*, 102.
12. *Ibid.*, 103.

Apart from meeting these (theological questions), theologians will bear a major responsibility to adapt codes of ethics and standards of value to an age where even the Eternal Verities are considered open to challenge.

Scientists themselves are, meanwhile, trying hard to build their own codes and standards out of logic and scientific knowledge. The growing movement is called Scientific Humanism, or sometimes Evolutionary Humanism. Influential on it have been such figures as the late French Jesuit scientist-philosopher, Pierre Teilhard de Chardin, and Sir Julian Huxley, who has outlined his version of Scientific Humanism in a book called Religion without Revelation.

Many biologists are hopeful that the revelations of biology itself will give us new and profound insights into the true nature of man, allowing us to draw up laws and ethical systems that are consistent with that nature. The New Man science helps create may also be much better equipped to deal with problems that now look insoluble, and the new powers we get may give us answers we cannot now predict—or may render some of the problems obsolete. So, even at a time when the daily newspapers are full of wars and riots and murders, and we despair that "human nature" can never be different, let us not give up hope yet. "Can the Ethiopian change his skin," asks Jeremiah, "or the leopard his spots? Then may ye also do good, that are accustomed to do evil." If it suddenly turns out that the Ethiopian and the leopard and you and I can change anything it pleases us to change, then it follows— does it not?—that even we may also do good?[13]

Man will change his nature and will then be able to do good because he, the new god by virtue of his biological revolution, will be good in all that he does. His will shall be *ipso facto* good. "We can guarantee that good will be done only by looking to it ourselves." "The time ahead is wild and uncharted" and only man can chart the way.[14]

---

13. *Ibid.*, 111.
14. *Idem.*

The presuppositions of this Scientific Humanism are evolutionary. For the evolutionary faith, there are no fixed boundaries in creation, only an evolutionary merging of one form into another. As a result, the line between man and the animals is not a fixed one; organs can be transplanted, embryos transplanted, and the genetic code used to make man into a new creature.

The whole position, however, rests on illusion. Tissue rejection is a major roadblock to success for these scientific dreamers. The body rejects foreign organs, foreign grafts, and works to destroy them. Man is a distinct creature, separate from all others, and all men have a biological individuality. Every body has a powerful defense system against invaders, whether disease-bearing bacteria or viruses. The body's cells, some fifty trillion, are all concerned with rejecting *any* invader. The blood's phagocytes also work to destroy the invader. Scientists have found this process of rejection so strong that, under a microscope, it is very apparent to the eye of the observer. But, it must be noted,

> Rejection of foreign cells is not the only barrier to transplant surgery. Drugs, X rays, even certain diseases can suppress the immune response and the graft will seemingly take—unless a paradoxical mechanism comes into play, in which the graft turns on its host and begins rejecting the body in which it has been placed. This reaction has been called "runt disease," a name coined by Dr. R. E. Billingham—one of the great modern transplant scientists—for the wasting effect it produces in the host animal.[15]

By means of radiation, the body's resistance to foreign cells can be subverted; low-energy radiation can destroy the blood's immunity to foreign bodies and make transplanting possible. This method, however, resulted in two problems. First, this destruction of immunity meant that there was no resistance to disease. The transplant would work for a time, but the host

---

[15.] Fred Warshofsky, *The Rebuilt Man: The Story of Spare-Parts Surgery* (New York: Thomas Y. Crowell, 1965), 49.

body eventually died of some ailment, as sniffles, for example, became a killing pneumonia because no immunity remained. Second, radiation, unless lethal, only temporarily "knocked out the rejection response."[16] Drugs have been used to produce the same effect, but, again, "The individual is left defenseless in an environment suddenly fraught with menace. But until someone finds a way to suppress only the response to the transplant antigen, the drug is the best hope for a successful transplant."[17] Experiments with immunization by means only of cells from donor animals are regarded as a more hopeful alternative.[18]

All these attempts have one thing in common, an evolutionary presupposition. According to Genesis 1:24, God made "every living creature after his kind." Instead of an open frontier, leading from one living creature to another, all merging upward and downward, all creatures are created by God after their kind, with relationships based on a common Creator and individualities based on being particular and specific creations. The attempt of evolutionary surgery to deny the distinctiveness of creatures or to overrule this individuality is doomed to fail. The experiments work against life rather than with it and for it. For scientific experimentation to work in favor of life requires a respect for life in all its forms as God made it. The present efforts attempt to thwart approaching death by techniques which ensure death. They involve the presupposition that man can become his own god and recreator and can also remake his own universe. We can agree with *Life* that these are "audacious experiments," but the ostensible "biological revolution" is instead a scientific blind alley.

---

16. *Ibid.*, 64.
17. *Ibid.*, 68.
18. *Ibid.*, 78 ff.

Chapter Five

The Premises
of Evolutionary Thought

Sigmund Freud, as an evolutionary scientist, has been a source of embarrassment to his many dedicated followers at one critical point: Freud grounded his evolutionary thinking on the theories of Lamarck. The inheritance of acquired characteristics is basic to Freud's anthropology, biology, and psychology. In the face of extensive criticism, Freud "adhered throughout his life" to "the Lamarckian belief."[1] At this point, even his devoted disciple and biographer, Dr. Ernest Jones, criticized Freud as "what one must call an obstinate adherent of this discredited Lamarckism."[2] Freud, however, was resolute. Because of his hostility to religion, the doctrine of evolution was intensely important to Freud, and evolutionary theory provided for no effective mechanism for evolution apart from Lamarck. To deny Lamarck and the inheritance of acquired characteristics was to posit a god-like power somewhere in or behind evolution and to introduce illegitimately an element resembling the supernatural. It pointed to an entelechy of being, a potentiality or power far

---

[1.] Ernest Jones, M.D., *The Life and Work of Sigmund Freud*, vol. I (New York: Basic Books, 1961), 347.
[2.] *Ibid.*, vol. II, 311.

exceeding the original elements of the universe. If *nothing is acquired*, then *everything* is *involved*, and what has evolved was originally involved in the original spark of energy or matter out of which all the universe has developed. Such an assumption would be ridiculous; it would place in that original atom powers commensurate with God. Freud saw only one consistent theory on which to ground his evolutionary faith: Lamarck's concept of acquired characteristics. Freud stated his thesis succinctly: "If nothing is acquired nothing can be inherited."[3] All of Freud's psychology rests on this concept of acquired characteristics. It is not our purpose here to analyze the implications of this position for Freud's psychoanalytic theory; this has been done in another context.[4] What does concern us is Freud's thesis: "If nothing is acquired nothing can be inherited." To introduce any other mechanism is to introduce the miraculous in disguise.

Freud's shrewd observation deserves renewed attention. The miraculous is indeed commonplace in evolutionary theory, although in a disguised manner. An important aspect of the standard evolutionary geological time table is the urgent necessity for countless millions of years to dilute the miracles of evolution and make them "natural." It is assumed that changes which are impossible or else miraculous when pinpointed in time can be rendered possible and natural when blanketed with millions of years. Given the millions of years, spontaneous generation is "naturalized" along with other steps in the evolution of species. *Philosophically*, the basic assumption of these positions is the inherent power of all being: the entire spectrum of nature has within itself a *being in process* of almost unlimited potentialities. This being in process has already manifested a measure of potentiality in the universe we know; there is no reason to suppose that its potentiality is exhausted or that somewhere continuous creation is not in process. This being, which is the whole of the natural world, possesses, therefore, whether consciously or

---

[3.] Jones, II, 333, 1955, 1962.
[4.] See R. J. Rushdoony, *Freud* (Vallecito, Calif.: Ross House Books, 1995).

not, and probably unconsciously, all the vast reservoir of power which orthodox Christianity has associated with God. In a sense, of course, the greater faith rests with the evolutionist in assuming that the order, structure, and design of creation is the product of a blind and unconscious potentiality rather than that of the totally self-conscious and ontological Trinity.

The implications of this position are especially of interest when we analyze the philosophical position of those who hold to creative evolution or progressive creationism. This compromising position represents an attempt by neo-evangelical Christians to retain the respectability of both science and Christianity. Basic to their position is the denial of the *creative act* in favor of a *creative process*. The six days of creation give way to the geological timetable, a substitute god of like creative power. But the moment creativity is transferred or to any degree ascribed to the process of being, to the inner powers of nature, to that extent sovereignty and power are transferred from God to Nature. Nature, having developed as a result of its creative process, contains within itself the laws of its being. God is an outsider to Nature, able to give inspiration to men within Nature, but unable to govern them because He is not their Creator and hence not their source of law. Of course, the creative evolutionist denies that he is surrendering God; he is trying to retain all the values of two systems of thought. But, in attempting to serve two masters, he is clearly being disloyal to one, since both have mutually exclusive claims. Where does creativity rest, within God or within Nature? If it rests in God, then the universe is, as Genesis 1 declares it to be, the result of a series of creative acts without process in the short span of six days, and all perfect and good. If creativity rests in Nature, then the universe is the result of a creative process, and the laws of its being and of its creatures are to be derived, not from an alien God who is an outsider, but from Nature itself. The creative evolutionist attempts to hold to either an outright dualism, and in every dualism one god becomes the evil god, or he

attempts to maintain the two in dialectical tension. It is not
without significance that virtually all progressive creationists,
while professing degrees of criticism of dialectical theology, do
nevertheless maintain a relatively appreciative and even
friendly attitude toward this radical departure from orthodox
Christianity. Indeed, progressive creationism or creative
evolution must be described as at least incipient dialectical
theology.

This was clearly apparent in the American Scientific
Affiliation symposium, edited by Russell L. Mixter, entitled
Evolution and Christian Thought Today (1959). The Thomistic
(or dialectic) nature of this symposium was cited by this writer
in a review article.[5] Such progressive creationist writers
commonly hold to a double-revelation theory, the revelation
of spiritual truths through the Bible by God, and the
revelation of God in nature. It is held that these two truths
cannot be in contradiction.[6] Basic to this double-revelation
theory is the Thomistic and Greek concept that the reason of
autonomous man is capable of impartially and objectively
investigating the truths of creation and of establishing them as
a valid revelation of nature. The source of "revelation"
concerning the universe is, then, man's reason and science. The
source of revelation concerning God and the supernatural is
the Bible. Reason and science can firmly establish truth in their
realm, the knowable, whereas the province of the Bible lies
beyond the natural world. To use the Bible as a source-book
for facts concerning nature and history is thus regarded as
illegitimate. Jan Lever has gone so far as to say "that we may
not consider the language of the Bible as scientifically
conceptual language; hence, we may never demand from
Scripture exact physical, astronomical, biological and thus also
not exact historical knowledge."[7] This position discludes from

---

[5] *Westminster Theological Journal* (November, 1960): 59-60.
[6] See John C. Whitcomb Jr., *The Origin of the Solar System, Biblical Iner-
rancy and the Double-Revelation Theory* (Philadelphia: Presbyterian and
Reformed Publishing Company, 1964). Adherents of the double-revelation theory are cited on 31 f.

history not only the prosaic account of Genesis 1, but also the accounts of the resurrection and the poetical narratives of the virgin birth. Such a view of the Bible is not Christian: it is dialectical, and the difference between these scholars and Karl Barth is only one of degree, not of kind.

Moreover, this dialectical position, by embracing two realms of truth, gives us two sets of infallible truth which cannot be attacked. Since the Bible is limited to revealing only spiritual truths, most of it is open, of course, to attack because its subject matter falls within the domain of science and history. What about evolution? Where lies its immunity? James O. Buswell III has given clear expression to this area of infallible truth:

> One of the chief drawbacks to the anti-evolutionists, from Darwin's early critics to the present day (familiar as some of their leaders are with the data), is that their activities and literature have been almost completely wrapped up in arguments over petty fragments of the record, assuming that to attack evolution as a total philosophy one must show the data upon which the assumptions are based to be untrue.[8]

This is an amazing statement. The data and facts of evolution can be untrue, but "the total philosophy" of evolution cannot be disproved, and it is wrong to assume that "to attack evolution as a total philosophy one must show the data upon which the assumptions are based to be untrue." What other resources does a scientist have? If fallacious and "untrue" data as the foundation of a theory fail to disprove that theory, what can be done? Buswell does not give an answer, but it is apparent that the double-revelation theory is implicit in this perspective. We have an area of immunity from disproof because it is an area of revelation.

---

7. Jan Lever (Peter G. Berkhout, M.D., translator), *Creation and Evolution* (Grand Rapids: International Publications, 1958), 171.
8. James O. Buswell III, in Russell L. Mister, editor, *Evolution and Christian Thought Today* (Grand Rapids: Eerdmans, 1959), 169.

The appearance of Darwin's thesis was the appearance of an alternative revelation to the Bible. According to George Bernard Shaw, "If you can realize how insufferably the world was oppressed by the notion that everything that happened was an arbitrary personal act of an arbitrary personal God of dangerous, jealous and cruel personal character, you will understand how the world jumped at Darwin."[9] Although Shaw's conception of God is a gross caricature, his basic analysis is correct. On the one hand, man faced an account of origins as the creative act of the ontological trinity, a totally self-conscious Person, omnipotent, omniscient, and sovereign, and to whom man is totally responsible. On the other hand, Darwinism offered an account of origins which performed all the miracles of creation and yet was totally impersonal, materialistic, and held no man to account. An unregenerate world jumped to it as "liberation." It provided, to cite the title of a modern book, a "god without thunder." In this evolutionary perspective, potentiality resides *within* the Universe, not beyond it in God. This position is an article of faith. A prominent philosopher, in discussing the question of origins, stated candidly that the philosophically astute naturalist will refuse to ask the question of origins: just as the Christian will take God and the Bible as his "given," so the pragmatic naturalist should insist on taking the world as it exists today and the concept of evolution as his "given," his basic assumption about reality.

The creative evolutionist holds a position which lacks the philosophical consistency of either the naturalist or the orthodox Christian: he attempts to operate in terms of two "givens" and to maintain them in dialectical tension. But every dialectical position, because it is an attempt to maintain and reconcile two mutually exclusive concepts or "givens," is ultimately doomed to resolve the tension in favor of one or the other. A dialectical position is precisely the insistence on

---

[9]. Cited by Arnold Lunn, in Introduction to *Is Evolution Proved? A Debate Between Douglas Dewar and H. S. Shelton* (London: Hollis and Carter, 1947), 4.

maintaining this hold on two warring concepts, and, while it is destined to collapse, it finds nothing more difficult to accept than this inevitable failure.

We thus have two rival faiths, each supporting a belief in miracles, one by God, the other by the potentiality inherent in the universe. We have a third position, the attempt to unite these two. But Freud's resort to Lamarck had as its motive a resolution that would avoid this dilemma of rival miracles. *Granted* the validity of acquired characteristics, then evolution is a thoroughly natural phenomenon. But here Freud introduced as much faith as he had rejected: the belief in acquired characteristics is a faith, and an amazing one. Systematically, according to this theory, from the beginning of time, important new characteristics have been acquired by various forms of being and have then been transmitted to successive forms of matter and then of life. These modifications are "induced by the action of environment."[10] Lamarckism is environmentalism, and while Lamarck is disowned, environmentalism is basic to many areas of study other than Freudian psychology, and the implicit Lamarckism in much evolutionary thought is considerable. The point which concerns us is the inescapable miracles built into this position as into every form of evolutionary thought.

God, clearly, is an inescapable premise of human thought. Man either faces a world of total chance and brute factuality, a world in which no fact has meaning and no fact has any relationship to any other fact, or else he accepts the world of God's creation and sovereign law. But men often refuse this choice. They deny the world of brute factuality, but they also openly deny God while trying to reintroduce all the attributes of God's creative power in naturalized form. They cannot escape God as a premise of their thinking, but they refuse to accept Him as God. Their science operates on borrowed premises, and their hypothesis conceals a hidden and utterly

[10.] Sir William Cecil Dampier, *A History of Science and Its Relations with Philosophy and Religion* (Cambridge: University Press, third edition, 1944), 294.

irrational miraculous power. If evolutionary scientists
eliminated this faith and confined themselves to the facts, they
would have no knowledge at all, only a vast ocean of
meaningless and unrelated facts which could not be made to
correspond except by positing a world of meaning whose
hidden premise is God. With Cornelius Van Til, we must
assert that, where it is consistently and rigorously applied,
"science is absolutely impossible on the non-Christian
principle."[11]

> An illustration may indicate more clearly what is meant.
> Suppose we think of a man made of water in an infinitely
> extended and bottomless ocean of water. Desiring to get
> out of water, he makes a ladder of water. He sets this
> ladder upon the water and against the water and then
> attempts to climb out of the water. So hopeless and
> senseless a picture must be drawn of the natural man's
> methodology based as it is upon the assumption that time
> or chance is ultimate. On his assumption his own
> rationality is a product of chance. On his assumption even
> the laws of logic which he employs are products of chance.
> The rationality and purpose that he may be searching for
> are still bound to be products of chance....
>
> It will then appear that Christian theism, which was first
> rejected because of its supposed authoritarian character, is
> the only position which gives human reason a field for
> successful operation and a method of true progress in
> knowledge.[12]

Only on the presupposition of Christian theism is a valid
science possible. The orthodox Christian holds that God as
Creator has created both the facts and the laws of physical
existence, so that the facts exist in the context of law. God
stands behind all creation as Creator and sustainer. He has, Van
Til points out, adapted "the laws of our minds" to the "laws of
the facts," so that the "knowledge that we have of the simplest
objects of the physical universe is still based upon the

---

11. Cornelius Van Til, *The Defense of the Faith* (Philadelphia: The Presbyterian and Reformed Publishing Company, 1955), 285.
12. *Ibid.*, 119.

revelational activity of God." Science is possible because the Biblical revelation is true.

> Thus the truth of Christianity appears to be the immediately indispensable presupposition of the fruitful study of nature. In the first place without it the physical scientist could have no assurance that his hypothesis would have any relevance to any of the facts in his field of study. For then Chance would be supreme. There would be no facts distinguishable from other facts. Unless the plan and therewith the interpretation or thought of God be back of all facts in their relations to all other facts, no idea, no hypothesis that the human mind could make with respect to them, would have any application to them.

> Secondly, except for the truth of Christianity it would be impossible to *exclude* one hypothesis rather than another. It would be impossible to exclude such ideas as would enter "into the minds of the insane." This second point is involved in the first.

> In the third place, without the truth of Christianity there would be no possibility of the testing of one hypothesis as over against another. The idea of testing hypotheses by means of "brute facts"...is meaningless. Brute facts, i.e., facts not created and controlled by God, are mute facts. They have no discernible character. They cannot, together, operate in regularity, thus forming a uniformity of nature. Thus they cannot constitute the reality which Christians and non-Christians know in common in order by it to test the "hypotheses" of the existence or the non-existence of God. It is the truth of Christianity alone that permits us to attach any significance to the idea of testing of an hypothesis.[13]

The non-Christian scientist is able to formulate and discover only because he operates on secretly Christian premises while denying that faith.[14] Factuality apart from God is totally meaningless factuality. "No fact, then, is truly known unless its createdness in the biblical sense is owned by the scientist,"[15] although this acceptance is generally unacknowledged.

---

13. *Ibid.*, 283 f.
14. R. J. Rushdoony, *By What Standard?* (Vallecito, Calif.: Ross House Books, 1995), 24.

But God remains as the inescapable premise of human thought. Because God is the Creator, every aspect of the universe and of man is structured by God's creative act and eternal decree, and therefore reflects His law and order. Men cannot escape Him nor can they shut Him out. If they attempt to think without Him as their premise, they simply reintroduce His attributes in the form of miraculous potentialities and processes which reduce science to irrationalism and self-contradiction.

---

15. Robert L. Reymond, *A Christian View of Modern Science* (Philadelphia: Presbyterian and Reformed Publishing Company, 1964), 10.

Chapter Six

The Necessity
for Creationism

When the first edition of Charles Darwin's *On the Origin of Species* was published on November 24, 1859, all 1,250 copies sold out on the day of publication. The world was waiting for a theory with scientific prestige to render the Bible and God obsolete, and men immediately jumped on the bandwagon of Darwinism. George Bernard Shaw described the relief of men at being rid of God and declared "the world jumped at Darwin."[1]

A great many churchmen climbed on that bandwagon then, and many more have done it since. The appeal is very great. Why not compromise? Why not be "scientific," or scientifically respectable? Since the *Genesis* account of creation is such a liability, why not concentrate on other matters of faith and accommodate the Bible to evolution? Why risk being considered ignorant and backward?

Bernard Ramm, in *The Christian View of Science and Scripture*, searched for "more credible, reasonable interpretations which should cause no embarrassment to any

---

[1.] Cited by Arnold Lunn, ed., in introduction, of Douglas Dewar, and H. S. Shelton, *Is Evolution Proved?* (London: Hollis and Carter, 1947), 4.

man with a scientific mentality but also with Christian convictions."[2] Ramm's purpose is to harmonize the Bible and modern science. Is such an approach tenable? Why defend old fashioned, strict creationism?

Saint James observed, "For whosoever shall keep the whole law, and yet offend in one point, he is guilty of all" (James 2:10). Similarly, anyone who denies the authority of Scripture at one point has denied it at all points. If we assert that we can set aside the six-day creation doctrine, we have asserted our supremacy over Scripture. *Our* mind and *our* convenience now have a higher authority than the Bible, so that we have totally denied its authority and asserted our own authority instead. If we claim the right at any point to set aside Scripture, we have established ourselves as the higher authority at *every* point. Clearly, therefore, the question of authority is at stake in Genesis 1: God or man? Whose word is authoritative and final?

But there is much more at stake. Science itself is involved. There are issues involved in creationism which are basic to the existence of science. Let us examine the necessity of creationism for science. Dr. Robert P. Knight, M.D., in his presidential address to the American Psychopathological Association (New York, May 9, 1946), stated:

> Determinism is a fundamental tenet of all science. Indeed, it is inconceivable that we could explain or count on anything in the physical world without relying on the basic assumption that all phenomena are strictly determined. Dynamic psychology is a science of human thinking and human behavior, and as a science must be deterministic. The phenomena of human thought, feeling, and behavior, of the whole range of personality development, in health and in psychopathology, must be understandable and explainable in terms of the causal factors of heredity, early psychological conditioning, subsequent life experiences, the composite of forces, external and internal, playing on the personality. In such a deterministic science of human behavior there is no place

---

[2.] Bernard Ramm, *The Christian View of Science and Scripture* (Grand Rapids, Michigan: Eerdmans, 1955), 168.

for the fortuitous, nor for "free will" in the sense used in philosophy. Whatever human actions or decisions seem to indicate the operation of a free will, or a freedom of choice, can be shown, on closer inspection and analysis, to be based on unconscious determinism. The causal factors were there and operative, but were simply not in the conscious awareness of the individual.[3]

Knight's conclusion is a very interesting one:

Determinism is a prerequisite of all science, including dynamic psychology. The alternative is not free will, but indeterminism, which implies chaos, unpredictability, and a denial of cause and effect relationships in human affairs. Free will is a subjective feeling, which is better called a sense of inner freedom, and which depends on harmony and integration of the personality. It is experienced by those psychologically healthy persons who willingly choose a course of action according to inner standards they are glad to obey. Psychotherapy, far from requiring freedom to choose in order to influence patients treated, itself operates deterministically to achieve for the patient this subjective sense of freedom.[4]

Without getting involved in a discussion of predestination versus determinism, we can observe that Knight has rightly seen that the issue is one between a world under absolute law and a world of chaos, and he sees a world of law and of cause and effect as basic to science. If chaos or chance be ultimate, then there can be no science. An absolute, determined order, Knight states, "is a fundamental tenet of all science...a prerequisite of all science."

But this statement points to a schizophrenic aspect of modern science. The theory of evolution requires a belief that somehow all things arose out of chance, out of "the fortuitous" which Knight condemns; evolutionary science denies spontaneous generation as a fact but requires it in theory in order to account for the universe. Thus, J. H. Rush, while unable to affirm spontaneous generation, places his hope in

---

[3.] Robert P. Knight, "Determinism, 'Freedom,' and Psychotherapy," *Psychiatry*, vol. IX, no. 3 (August 1946): 251.

[4.] *Ibid.*, 262.

finding evidence of it and writes: "It would be satisfying to find some kind of life on another planet, even lowly forms, to support our basic thesis that life is a spontaneously originating process."[5]

Science thus *wants* a universe of law and of causality without God, and it would rather ascribe all the magnificent order of the universe to chaos rather than to God, because scientists are *fallen* men, men in rebellion against God and bent on suppressing their knowledge of Him.

Men will either presuppose God, or they will presuppose themselves as the basic reality of being. If they assume themselves to be autonomous and independent from God, they will then wage war against God at every point. There is no such thing as an area of neutrality: men will either affirm God at every point in their lives and thinking, or else they will deny Him at every point. As Dr. Cornelius Van Til has observed:

> Now if our contention that the evolution-hypothesis is a part of an antitheistic theory of reality is correct, then we must do away with every easy-going attitude. The evolutionist is then a soldier in that great, that seemingly all-powerful army of antitheists that has from time immemorial sought to destroy the people of God. We must then prepare for a life and death struggle if not in the courts of the land then in the higher courts of human thought.
>
> ...Every time any human being opens his mouth to say anything he either says that God is or that God is not a reality. It could not be otherwise. God claims to control every fact.[6]

Since God created all things, nothing can be truly understood apart from Him, and no fact can be truly interpreted apart from Him. When men seek to give an atheistic or agnostic

---

5. J. H. Rush, *The Dawn of Life* (Garden City, N.Y.: Hanover House, 1957), 213; cf. 63.

6. Cornelius Van Til, "Our Attitude Toward Evolution," in *The Banner*, 11 December 1931, reproduced in Van Til, *Science Articles* (Philadelphia: Westminster Theological Seminary), 12.

interpretation to any fact, it is because they are at war with God and are bent on denying Him.

The basis of evolutionary theories is this anti-God position of apostate and fallen man. The convincing thing about evolution is not that it proves man's origins or even gives anything resembling a possible theory, but that it dispenses with God. Scientists themselves have often called attention to the absurdities of evolutionary theory. Consider, for example, the comments of G. A. Kerkut, a biochemist:

> It is a matter of faith on the part of the biologist that biogenesis did occur and he can choose whatever method of biogenesis happens to suit him personally; the evidence for what did happen is not available.
>
> It seems at times as if many of our modern writers on evolution have had their views by some sort of revelation....[7]

This does not mean that Kerkut accepts creationism. Apparently any alternative other than God is preferable to evolutionists. Kerkut's hope is that "future experimental work"[8] will provide an answer, but he is already sure that the answer will be some form of evolution. Thus, his basic assumption is a religious faith that the answer is not God, but something else, although he does not know what that something is! Evolution is not a science but a religious faith which has taken over the sciences and rules them dogmatically.

And yet evolution, which rests on chaos, is supported by men whose sciences presuppose God and His eternal decree. Evolution requires chance, whereas science rests on absolutely determined factors and on causality. The doctrine of evolution is thus basically hostile to science.

Again, evolution is a theory which is radically hostile to Biblical religion. The Bible clearly asserts that God created heaven and earth, the whole created universe, in six days. If

---

[7.] G. A. Kerkut, *Implications of Evolution* (Oxford: Pergamon Press, 1965), 150, 155.
[8.] *Ibid.*, 157.

this statement be allegorized or interpreted away, no meaning stands in Scripture. Because God created all things, He and He alone is the sustainer, governor, and redeemer of all things. Man is responsible to God *because* God is his maker, because man is totally God's creation and therefore totally under God's law. God is man's savior because God as creator is alone omnipotent over man and the universe and sufficient for all things. God is man's judge because He is man's creator, and He created man for His own purposes and glory. If God's creative work is denied, then God's governance and redemption are also denied, because God is made irrelevant to man and to the universe, or at least no longer omnipotent over them. *Every* doctrine of Scripture is undermined when strict creationism is undermined. Wherever strict creationism is set aside, the vital nerve of Christianity is cut, and the church begins to move in terms of humanistic and political power rather than the power of God.

The alternative to creationism is evolution, and Darwin has led to Marx and Freud, to materialism and agnosticism, and, as M. Stanton Evans has noted, to the "annihilation of value derived from Nietzche and James and Dewey. These are the root precepts of Liberal philosophy."[9] The problem of our time is not material: it is spiritual. Technology has given man more material wealth than he has ever before possessed, but man's condition is regularly described as a desperate one, and man lives in a chronic state of anxiety. What the doctrine of evolution has done is to destroy man, not God. A theory cannot alter ultimate reality; it can affect the mind and welfare of man. How has it done so?

First of all, man is no longer viewed as created in the image of God. According to Scripture, man was created in God's image, and, although fallen, is strictly under God's law. Man cannot be reduced to the level of an animal. The Sabbath was made for man, not man for the Sabbath. Man is called to glorify God and to enjoy Him forever, and the world is man's

---

9. M. Stanton Evans, *The Liberal Establishment* (New York: Devin Adair, 1965), 178f.

dominion under God. But the evolutionary theory views man as a product of the world rather than a destined lord over it in Christ. Man is seen as having evolved out of the fortuitous concourse of atoms and out of primeval slime. Instead of being set over nature, man is set under nature as a product of it. Man is reduced to the same slavish status as existed during antiquity in ancient Egypt and other states which held to an evolutionary model. Man's liberty is a product of Biblical faith; the concept of evolution produces slavery, and it was welcomed by Marx as the necessary foundation for socialism. When man is a product of nature, as he is according to theories of evolution, he is passive in relationship to nature; his being is determined by nature, and his psychology is passive, conditioned, reflex action rather than governing action. When man knows himself to be created by God, and his faith is basic to his thinking, man is a product of God's creative work and is therefore passive in relationship to God but active towards nature. He is determined by God, not by nature, and man is then active towards nature and governs it. Man is thus free from nature, not a slave to it, because man is created and governed by God, not by nature. Man's calling is to exercise dominion under God over nature, to rule it, develop and exploit it, under God and to His glory. Only the regenerate man in Jesus Christ can do this. The fallen man is in captivity to his own nature and to the forces around him. As a result, liberty rapidly declines when Biblical Christianity declines. Where men are not ruled by God, they are ruled by tyrants. And the rise of evolutionary thinking has produced a world-wide rise of totalitarianism. Since man is no longer seen as God's creation, he is becoming a creature of the total state, and the total state is determined to remake man in its own image. In consequence, man is now the primary experimental animal. People are alarmed at the use of animals in scientific experimentation. But the grim reality is that the primary experimental animal is man. Not only the mental health experts, but also virtually every agency of civil government is today engaged in trying to remake man. Moreover, scientists are engaged in experiments concerning psycho-chemical and electronic controls over man. Such experiments were reported in *Life* magazine, March 8 and 15, 1963.[10] Scientists talk seriously, as did C. R. Schafer, at the National Electronics Conference at the Illinois Institute of Technology, about enslaving men with built-in electronic controls, a socket mounted under the scalp "a few months after birth," with "electrodes reaching selected areas of the brain tissue." After "a year or two...a miniature radio receiver and antenna" would be "plugged into the socket," and from that time on the child would be modified "or completely controlled by bio-electric signals radiated from state-controlled transmitters."[11] When they *begin* by talking and experimenting in this vein, as they have done, we can be sure that the *conclusion* of their thinking will be far worse. Orwell's *1984* will look like paradise compared to what these evolutionists plan to do with man. When men set aside God as Creator, they then set themselves up as man's recreators, as the new gods over man and the universe. It was this same temper which characterized man before the Flood, and Genesis 6:5 declares, "And God saw that the wickedness of man was very great in the earth, and that every imagination of the thoughts of his heart was only evil continually."

A second way in which evolutionary theory has altered the mind of man is with respect to responsibility. According to Scripture, man is a responsible creature; his responsibility is to serve and glorify God; failing to do this, man became a sinner, sentenced to death. Evolutionary theory, because it sees man as a product of nature, sees man, not as a responsible creature made in the likeness of God, but as a product of a long evolutionary history and environment. As a result, man is not responsible; he is not a sinner but a victim. He is what his environment has made him. The means, therefore, of changing

---

[10.] Robert Coughlan, "Part I, Behavior by Electronics," *Life*, vol. 54, no. 10, 8 March 1963, 90-106; Robert Coughlan, "Control of the Brain, Part II, The Chemical Mind-Changers," *Life*, vol. 54, no. 11, 15 March 1963, 81-94.

[11.] San Francisco *Chronicle*, 7 October 1956, 4.

man is not regeneration, not moral responsibility and renewal, but changing his environment. Man has to be *reconditioned*. This means a Pavlovian world. Even as Pavlov trained his dogs to salivate when he rang a bell, so man has to be trained, like any animal, by conditioning. This means that education ceases to be education: it becomes brainwashing and conditioning. And thus responsibility disappears. After all, it is not the criminal's fault, it is society's fault; it is not the young delinquent's fault, it is his family's fault. Mothers, as a result, are extensively blamed for their children's sins and failures, or for their mental collapse. As one psychiatrist, Dr. Humphrey Osmond, M.D., has noted:

> And if Mama was not to blame, the myth goes on, it must be papa, or the husband or wife. This can be extended *and is extended* to anything in the family background— poverty, riches, lack of discipline, too much discipline.

> Thus far, however, no one has blamed sons and daughters for the schizophrenia of Mama and Papa. But parents may have senile psychosis, and the day may come when children will be blamed for that.

> *It is dangerous these days to be the relative of a person who is mentally ill for you will probably be blamed for driving him mad.*[12]

This trend to blame someone or something else will not be stopped by such common sense observations by a few dissenting psychiatrists. Environmentalism is a logical necessity for evolutionary thinking. The theory holds that man is a product of his geological and biological environment, and, because evolution is a continuing process, not a finished act, this means that man is still a product of his environment. As a result, the consistent evolutionist will, first, insist that the environment is responsible for man, not man for his environment. Second, he will try to provide the right biological and social environment to further man's evolution and to

---

[12] Dr. Humphrey Osmond, M.D., in "Postscript" to Gregory Stefan, *In Search of Sanity, the Journal of a Schizophrenic* (New Hyde Park, N.Y.: University Books, 1966), 244 f.

prevent man's devolution. This means total control over man, supposedly for man's welfare. Again we face the inescapable fact that evolutionary thinking *requires* totalitarianism. If the education of a people is dedicated to teaching evolution, it will also teach socialism or communism. Karl Marx knew better than others that evolution was a necessity for communism's success: it made socialism "scientific." *If men put their faith in evolution, they will then look to scientific socialist planners for salvation, rather than to Jesus Christ.* Their maker is their savior. Fredrich Engels agreed with Marx that Darwin's theory was basic to scientific socialism.[13]

When man is regarded as a product of his environment rather than a creature responsible to God, he ceases to be of much importance, either as a person or in his own thinking. Darwin himself doubted the validity of many aspects of his evolutionary model. For example, while denying all revelation, he believed that it seemed reasonable to conclude, "that the Universe is not the result of chance," even though his theory did so much to enthrone chance. He added,

> But then with me the horrid doubt always arises whether the convictions of man's mind, which has been developed from the mind of the lower animals, are of any value or at all trustworthy. Would any one trust in the convictions of a monkey's mind, if there are any convictions in such a mind?[14]

Darwin thus professed little respect for his own intellect. It is not surprising then that he had little respect for some races. He believed that some would be eliminated, and wrote, "Looking to the world at no very distant date, what an endless number of the lower races will have been eliminated by the higher civilized races throughout the world."[15] In other words, Darwin felt that evolution would eliminate "lower races." This

---

[13]. John N. Moore, "Evolution, Marxism, and Communism," *Creation Research Society*, out of print.

[14]. Letter of C. Darwin to W. Graham, 3 July 1881, in Francis Darwin, editor, *The Life and Letters of Charles Darwin*, vol. I (New York: Basic Books, 1959), 285.

[15]. *Ibid.*, I, 286.

is one possible approach to the "problem" from the evolutionary perspective: weed them out. The other approach is equally deadly: since environment changes men, provide these "lower races" with a new environment, new education, and a new set of controls, and you will quickly evolve them to the same level as that of what Darwin termed "the higher civilized races." Both of these evolutionary approaches reveal a fundamental contempt for man and a readiness to use him experimentally. More importantly, they shift the problem from faith and character to planning and control, from responsibility to conditioning and experimentation.

A third way in which evolutionary thinking has affected the minds of men is that it has given men a new religion, and that new religion is science. As C. F. Weizsacker observed at a scientific gathering:

> Science today is the only thing in which men as a whole believe: it is the only universal religion of our time.... The scientist has thus got himself into an ambiguous position: he is a priest of this new religion, possessing its secrets and marvels; for what to others is puzzling, strange or secret is plain to him. It is suddenly clear in many countries that the future of a nation, of a continent, of a view of life depends on producing enough scientists. Is this immoderate faith in the power of science justified?[16]

One of the clearest bits of evidence that science is now man's universal religion is the history of the churches since Darwin. Modernism is simply an attempt to keep religion up-to-date with science and philosophy. Even within supposedly evangelical circles, we see men like Ramm seeking harmony with science. *Genesis* is interpreted by most commentators, not in terms of what the Hebrew text requires, but in terms of evolutionary geology. When even the churches move so extensively in terms of the authority of the evolutionary

---

[16.] C. F. Weizsacker, *Reports of Geigy Bicentenary Scientific Day*, Basel, Switzerland, 3 June 1958, quoted in Evan Shute, *Flaws in the Theory of Evolution*, 228, (London, Canada: The Temside Press, 1961), 228. Reprinted in 1966 by The Craig Press, Nutley, N.J.

scientist, how much more so does the world bow down before this new priesthood!

And evolutionary science is a religion, and it speaks religiously, not scientifically. Its champions advocate evolution because they want to escape God and creationism. They deny purpose, meaning, and design in the world, because they cannot tolerate God and His creative law. A German scientists Du Bois-Reymond, has said:

> Here is the knot, here the great difficulty that tortures the intellect which would understand the world. Whoever does not place all activity wholesale under the sway of Epicurean chance, whoever gives only his little finger to teleology, will inevitably arrive at Paley's discarded "Natural Theology," and so much more necessarily, the more clearly he thinks and the most independent his judgment...the physiologist may define his science as a doctrine of the changes which take place in organisms from internal cause.... No sooner has he, so to speak, turned his back on himself than he discovers himself talking again of functions, performances, actions, and purposes of the organs. *The possibility ever so distant, of banishing from nature its seeming purpose, and putting a blind necessity everywhere in the place of final causes, appears, therefore, as one of the greatest advances in the world of thought*, from which a new era will be dated in the treatment of these problems. To have somewhat eased the torture of the intellect which ponders over the world-problem will, as long as philosophical naturalists exist, be Charles Darwin's greatest title to glory.[17]

The argument is clear-cut. Chance is affirmed as the mechanism of evolution in order to avoid God. The world shows design and purpose, not chance, *but chance is a religious necessity*, and this is, as Du Bois-Reymond noted, "Charles Darwin's greatest title to glory:" that he offered a theory which maintained that chance could be the mechanism of evolution. In other words, evolution is not even remotely connected with

---

[17.] Du Bois-Reymond, "Darwin Versus Faliani," quoted in Merz, *History of European Thought in the Nineteenth Century*, vol. II, 435.

scientific fact: it is a religious trick and device to escape from God.

A fourth way in which evolutionary thinking has affected the minds of men is in the area of morality. Biblical morality declares the sovereign authority of God and establishes His clear-cut commandments for men. Morality thus has reality; it is grounded in ultimate reality; it rests on the truth of God's Word and has the authority of God's judgment behind it. The theory of evolution has no moral absolutes. Morality, like man, is a product of evolution; it represents not ultimate and absolute truth, but social mores and customs. The new morality is the logical result of evolutionary theory. It simply wipes out all moral standards. The champions of the new morality declare that anything done "by mutual consent should not be prohibited by law" and is morally legitimate. The only crime is said to be compulsion or force used against another person. According to the "Bruins for Voluntary Parenthood and Sexual Liberty," in a 1966 hand-out at University of California at Los Angeles, "Where there is no victim, every act is morally right," and virtually every form of perversion is then listed and defended. But why limit lawful acts to voluntary acts? After all, if, as such persons believe, there is no ultimate truth, no ultimate right and wrong, why not regard force and consent as equally good? The Marquis de Sade was more logical here: for him, the only real crime was Christianity; all else was permissible, every sexual crime, theft, and even murder. "Can we possibly imagine Nature giving us the possibility of committing a crime which would offend her?"[18] At least one killer of late has been motivated in part by the Marquis de Sade's writings. A murderer in England, who boasted of several brutal murders, was a professed follower of the degenerate Marquis.[19] It is ridiculous to believe that, when

---

[18.] Leonard de Saint-Yves, editor, *Selected Writings of De Sade* (New York: British Book Centre, 1954), 258; cf. intro., 215 f., 237, 248, 253, 256, 266. See also Richard Seaver and Austryn Wainhouse, *The Marquis de Sade...Writings* (New York: Grove Press, 1965).

[19.] "Lewd Photos of Dead British Girl Shown," Santa Ana, California, *Register*, 9 December 1965.

men believe that every kind of act is morally legitimate and natural, they will not begin to practice many of these acts. And this is exactly what is happening all around us. The growing incidence of every kind of perversion and crime is a witness to this moral collapse. Sigmund Freud knew that total breakdown of all law and order could easily follow the widespread adoption of unbelief. When the masses become as atheistic as their leaders, Freud feared that they "[would] certainly kill without hesitation.... And so follows the necessity for either the most rigorous suppression of these dangerous masses and the most careful exclusion of all opportunities for mental awakening, or a fundamental revision of the relation between culture and religion."[20] In other words, Freud saw the solution, as he proceeded to develop it, as one of total control in the scientific socialist state. Either that, or atheism would lead to mass murder and total lawlessness.

Unfortunately, both socialism and moral breakdown accompanied by flagrant lawlessness are increasingly the result of our evolutionary thinking. Because God's moral law is denied, men are ever more inclined to live in terms of their sinful nature and their lawless demands for self-satisfaction. In a recent article on a New York City detective, George Barrett, the author reported on the collapse of law and order as seen from Barrett's perspective.

> If Barrett hates the bad guys, he grieves for the good. He walks through the west side of the precinct, among the crowded apartment houses, and he points to the heavy wire screens and bars covering the back windows over the alleys and empty lots. "Look at that," he says. "They have to make prisons for themselves to keep the germs out. They have to hide themselves behind bars."[21]

---

20. Sigmund Freud, *The Future of an Illusion* (Garden City, N.Y.: Double-day Anchor Books), 69 f.
21. James Miles, "The Detective," condensed from *Life*, 3 December 1966, in *Reader's Digest*, February 1967, 245.

In many cities today, similar conditions prevail: the good citizens make prisons of their own homes to protect themselves from the hoodlums who rule the streets. One prominent oil man commented on the moral breakdown by observing that backward areas of the world, which fifty years ago were the less safe areas for travel, are now safer than the streets of America. The reason for this is not that these areas have improved; they have not. It is because the total moral nihilism and anarchism of evolutionary thinking is creating a monstrous new barbarian who respects nothing and delights in destruction. Concerning such a man, David wrote, in Psalm 36: 1-2: "There is no dread of God before his eyes. For he flatters himself in his own thinking that his iniquity will not be found out or hated."[22] This new barbarianism will continue to increase until creationism is again believed, and, with it, Biblical Christianity and Christian moral order again prevail.

Jose Ortega y Gasset termed the specialized scientist of our day a barbarian:

> But if the specialist is ignorant of the inner philosophy of the science he cultivates, he is much more radically ignorant of the historical conditions requisite for its continuation; that is to say: How society and the heart of man are to be organized in order that there may continue to be investigators.... He also believes that civilization is there in just the same way as the earth's crust and the forest primeval.[23]

Modern men, scientists and humble believers in evolution alike, are parasites. They are living off the unearned capital of Christian civilization, on the impetus, law, and order of centuries of Christianity. Like all parasites, they are destroying the host body, Christendom, and its collapse will be their death also. They are denying the eternal decree of God, His sovereign and omnipotent creative counsel and decree, and as a result they are left with a world of chaos which is destructive

---

[22.] H. C. Leupold's translation in *Exposition of the Psalms* (Columbus, Ohio: Wartburg Press, 1959), 293.

[23.] Jose Ortega y Gasset, *The Revolt of the Masses* (New York: W. W. Norton, 1932), 216.

of science. If they were faithful to their philosophy, these scientists could have no science, because they would have to say that the world is a world of brute factuality without meaning, purpose, causality, or law. Every time a scientist works in his laboratory, he assumes the reality of God even though he denies God with his lips. He is thus destroying the very foundation of his science when he denies the God who created all things and who is the source of all law and all interpretation. The moral capital of Christendom is rapidly disappearing; if it disappears entirely, all culture and civilization will go with it, and the decline and fall of the West will be more devastating than the decline and fall of Rome.

The only alternative to this decline and fall is a renewal of Biblical Christianity, which requires a return to creationism. This means renouncing any philosophy, study, or science which seeks to act in complete independence of God. It means renouncing the idea of brute factuality, that is, the idea that facts exist apart from God and apart from any interpretation. Because God has created every fact in the universe, every fact must be understood in terms of the interpretation placed upon it by God's creative purpose. We must strive in every area to think God's thoughts after Him. We must believe that, in every area, there are God-ordained truths for man to know, and no other kind of fact and truth exists, only those created by God. Evolution says that the universe represents no purpose, plan, or law: it just happened. When we begin with such a total negation, we can only end up with a total negation. As Van Til has observed, a million zeroes still add up only to zero. And, because its social and cultural efforts are increasingly being reduced to the chaos and anarchy of a moral zero and, worse than that, a moral minus, it is an especially deadly moral chaos. This moral chaos is prowling our streets, pounding on our doors, and invading our homes. Scientific planning and mental health programs will not cure it: they are merely "scientific" forms of quackery which aggravate rather than alleviate the evil. The answer is a return to Biblical Christianity, Biblical creationism, to that faith defined by

Hebrews 11:3: "Through faith we understand that the worlds were framed by the word of God, so that things which are seen were not made of things which do appear." This is the basic truth which *all* men as God's creatures know, but, as Saint Paul declared, according to the original Greek, they "hold down the truth in unrighteousness" (Romans 1:18); they suppress this truth because of their sin, "For the invisible things of him from the creation of the world are clearly seen, being understood by the things that are made, even his eternal power and Godhead; so that they are without excuse" (Romans 1:20). Not only is creationism a *necessary* faith, *it is also an inescapable fact.*

Chapter Seven

The Act of Creation

The offense of Scripture is felt with especial intensity in our time with reference to the doctrine of creation. Academic respectability could no doubt be gained, and the tension with modern scientists lessened, if somehow the Genesis account could be read in terms which would make possible an accord with geological hypotheses and still maintain, in some fashion, an ostensibly Biblical theology. In recent years, such studies have been especially numerous.[1] Some of these attempts seek to be exegetical, pitting various expressions and phrases against the primary and open sense of Genesis 1. Others simply cast

---

[1.] See N. H. Ridderbos, *Is There a Conflict Between Genesis and Natural Science?* (Grand Rapids: Eerdmans, 1957); Jan Lever, *Creation and Evolution* (Grand Rapids: International, 1958); Bernard Ramm, *The Christian View of Science and Scripture* (Eerdmans: 1955); Russell L. Mixter, ed., *Evolution and Christian Thought Today* (Eerdmans: 1959); Meredith G. Kline, "Because It Had Not Rained," Westminster Theological Journal, II (May 1958): 2, 146-157. The present writer does not hesitate to add that, as one who grew up believing in evolution as "reconciled" to Christianity, and who attended a modernist seminary, he attempted, in discarding evolution as a culture-myth, to read the Genesis account in terms which were similar to these harmonistic attempts. This effort was finally discarded as it became increasingly apparent, with every such theory, that the plain meaning of Scripture made them hopelessly untenable, that, in short, one either accepts the miraculous creative act, or else the whole exegesis of Scripture is left open to stretching, allegorization, and accommodation of the most wretched sort.

exegesis out entirely, as do the writers of the American Scientific Affiliation in *Evolution and Christian Thought Today*, by declaring the Genesis account to be "poetic."[2] There is a singular absence of "poetry" in Genesis 1, which is rather declarative. Moreover, if "poetry" militates against accuracy or historicity, then Luke's account of the virgin birth must be reduced to myth.

The basic issue with reference to Genesis 1 was well stated by Keil and Delitzsch: "Creation is an act of the personal God, not a process of nature."[3] All harmonistic efforts have in common the desire to reduce creation to process and thereby make it amenable to the apostate science of autonomous man. In a mature creation, the priority of *act* over *process* means the priority of an external and sovereign decree of God to the inner workings and development of nature. The entire natural order is irrevocably placed in subordination to *decree* rather than to *process*, and this is a death sentence to current scientific theory. Only if the natural order, either through the entelechy of its being or through chance and natural selection, has by process and becoming entered into its being, can the autonomy and integrity of man and his order be preserved against the eternal decree. A mature creation is the product of a sovereign God and an absolute decree, and unavoidably makes the ultimate frame of reference transcendental, rather than immanent. Immanence requires process, and process leads to an ever-increasing emphasis on immanence. Scripture never speaks of biological *development*, but only of degeneration, a waxing old of creation. Biblical maturation is in terms of epistemological self-consciousness, cultural, historical, psychological and philosophical.

In terms of any consistent religion, a faith in process can *recognize* the existence of a god or a supreme being without feeling any necessity to worship him. To begin with a relatively modern illustration, the knowledge by American

---

[2]. Mixter, *op. cit.*, Hearn and Hendry, 67f.; Schweitzer, 47.
[3]. C. F. Keil and F. Delitzsch, *The Pentateuch*, vol. I (Eerdmans, 1949), 41.

Indians of a supreme being has been no small matter of debate. The Deists, with their theories of natural religion, were certain that the American Indians worshiped the "Great Spirit" and quickly reported such a faith. The anthropologists of the nineteenth and twentieth centuries, in reporting cultic practices, could only cite religious veneration of or association to natural forces, the wolf cult, the spirits of the dead, and similar cultic powers. Accordingly, many decided that no recognition of a supreme being existed among these tribes. In both approaches, a partial report is the basis of the conflict. The American Indians *knew* of a supreme being, but, contrary to the Deists, they did not *worship* him. His existence was accorded *recognition; he was not a proper object of worship.* As Wyman has stated, with reference to the Navaho, "man has his place in the universal continuum and if he misbehaves with respect to the traditional restrictions on human behavior in relation to the 'supernatural' there is a breakdown in a harmonious balance of things, resulting usually in illness of the transgressor or future illness of his or her unborn child."[4] Two essential points stand out clearly: (1) man is part of "the eternal continuum" and process, the principle of continuity, and (2) his necessary social and religious life requires a proper relation to all else, especially to the contiguous, i.e., that which is immediately next to, above, and below him, the principle of contiguity. Accordingly, worship was given to the *immediate natural forces* as the relevant powers, in that the awareness religiously of *creation as process rather than act* made, for example, the sun and rain relevant to agricultural tribes and the wolf and coyote to hunting tribes. The supreme being, as remote, was recognized but not worshiped. *Continuity* was essential. Thus, as Titiev has pointed out, the cult of the dead was important to Hopi religion, the dead being, while more powerful, still in continuity with their living society. "In every ceremony, therefore, the cult of the dead plays an important

---

[4.] Leland Clifton Wyman, "The Religion of the Navaho Indians," in Vergilius Ferm, ed., *Ancient Religions* (New York: The Philosophical Library, 1950), 344.

part."[5] The dead are thus far more important religiously than is a supreme being. The "gods" thus of man's religion are inevitably anthropomorphic in that they are created in man's image as seen in terms of process and as an aspect of nature. Whenever these religions have been "spiritualized" and made less continuous with man, they have rapidly eroded, as did Greek religion, into a philosophy which sophisticates the gods only to make, by virtue of the process, man's autonomy of the eternal decree all the more radical and naive. Continuity and contiguity are essential, or the false gods go, to be replaced by others.

These gods, natural forces, totems, and spirits constitute a form of *Baalim* very closely related to that which, in developed form, was denounced by God as a culminating abomination in Canaan. Canaanite religion was the religious development of the idea of process to its logical and emotional limits. The *Baalim* were lords, possessors, masters, the spiritual as well as actual *immediate powers* over man in this great hierarchy of being whose orderly process required the religious and sociological observance of hierarchial order in the great chain. "There was no such thing as a god Ba'al,"[6] for the reference was to the immediate proprietor or lord in matters spiritual, and a variety of such lords affected the life of every man. Since nature was conceived of as a process (to the extent that hard and fast lines between man and animal were not recognized), the essence of man's life was to advance himself within the framework of process. Man's indebtedness was in a double direction, upwards and downwards, and hence religions of process maintain fraternal relations in both directions, to both lords and "servants," as well as to both good and evil powers, so that the demonic power could also be worshiped. The tree served man, but man venerated the tree and kept peace in all directions as the means of advancing the process of being. Moreover, since process moves from the lesser to the greater,

---

[5] Mischa Titiev, "The Religion of the Hopi Indians," in Ferm, 376.
[6] Lewis Bayles Paton, "Baal, Beel, Bal," in James Hastings, ed., ERE, II, 285.

from the void to the form, from chaos to order, it follows that the *source* of power is in the lesser, the void, and in chaos, so that the various forms of Saturnalia enthrone the thief, the beggar, the violent criminal, and total chaos as instruments of *social regeneration.* As Caillois has pointed out, the very societies which emphasize *unified continuity* see periodic ritual chaos as the means to the golden age, and "the primordial chaos" is re-enacted as a regenerating force in Saturnalias. "In fact, the festival is presented as a re-enactment of the first days of the universe, the *Urzeit*, the eminently creative era...."[7] "The festival is thus celebrated in the context of the myth and assumes the function of regenerating the world."[8] Among the Jews, the indirect but real influence of this faith became apparent in the Talmudic requirement of Purim, when one must drink until distinction between the two cries, "May Haman be accursed," and "May Mordecai be blessed," becomes impossible. The return to chaos is the obliteration of good and evil in the name of process and the inherent power of process, which is beyond good and evil. Order constitutes a development in need of revitalization through orgy and regeneration, through the ritual baptism in chaos. Hence the sexual coition with animals, so strongly condemned by Scripture and under sentence of death to man and animal (Ex. 22:18; Lev. 18:23; 20:15-16), was a *ritual* act in such religions. Its *sub rosa* revival in the modern world is significant, as is its inclusion as one of "the six types of sexual activity" by Kinsey: "masturbation, spontaneous nocturnal emissions, petting, heterosexual intercourse, homosexual contacts and animal contact." All are deemed equally natural and hence equally normal.[9] *Integration downward into the all-powerful void* becomes a logical concomitant of the religion of process. The blunt supernaturalism of Scripture, with its ascription of power to God and direction to the eternal decree, is a standing

---

[7.] Roger Caillois, *Man and the Sacred* (Glencoe, Ill.: The Free Press, 1959), 103.

[8.] *Ibid.*, 108.

[9.] Edmund Bergler, M.D., *Homosexuality: Disease or Way of Life?* (New York: Hill and Wang, 1957), 178.

offense to those who want to see an immanent power and decree in nature.

How *process* assimilates ostensibly Biblical religion is tellingly seen in Theodore H. Gaster, who can speak of Canaanite religion as the religion of Israel: "Refined in the crucible of their own genius, it is this religion that they have passed down to us in the legacy of the Old Testament."[10] His concluding paragraph is especially revealing:

> Above all, however, Canaanite religion possesses its own permanent values, and to dismiss it as a mere heathen abomination is to allow the bias and censure of its enemies to take the place of objective judgment. One light differeth from another in glory, and if the faith of Israel is the sun in the firmament of ancient religious thought, that of Canaan is none the less a shining star. Canaanite religion takes us back into a world of thought and feeling informed by concepts and insights which are none the less precious for having been overborne and overswept in the onrushing tide of history. Here is an approach to the world and its fashion which establishes an intimacy between man and nature such as a mechanical age is apt to obliterate; which validates human existence by making man a necessary agent in the continuous process of creation; which substitutes for the humiliation of dependence the proud status of a co-worker with God. If its forms of expression are crude and its philosophy too immature to satisfy the requirements of a more refined metaphysic, that is only because it issues from the bright intuitions of the world's youth rather than from the clouded experience of its tired old age. Canaanite religion is assuredly one of the many mansions in the Father's house.[11]

In this statement concerning the "precious" religion of Canaan, several things are asserted very clearly:

(1) The intimacy and continuity between man and nature is affirmed.

---

10. Theodore H. Gaster, "The Religion of the Canaanite Religion," in Ferm, 114.
11. *Ibid.*, 140.

(2) Human experience is validated when man is made "a necessary agent in the continuous process of creation."

(3) This results in the substitution of "the proud status of a coworker with God" for "the humiliation of dependence."

Thus, a hierarchical religion, which affirms process and venerates immediate powers, spirits, or saints as ostensibly a humbler faith, is, when clearly seen, an exaltation of man to the status of "co-worker with God" in shaping creation. The hierarchy of being, whether in Canaan, Rome, evolutionary theories, or harmonistic movement within the camp of orthodoxy, is an instrument whereby the eternal decree is undermined by the priority of process, and man is exalted as one of the agents of process. Maturation is conceived as the product of *process*, and God's eternal decree as the source of a *mature* creation which is fallen and *in rebellion*, rather than in the process of maturation is denied.

The Biblical faith is in creation as a *divine act*, not *process*. *Process* means positing either an entelechy in nature, a continuum of inherent movement, or the positing of an inherent power which comes to maturation through chance and natural selection. This is the religion of Canaan, which did not *deny* Jehovah, but rather ignored Him. This *continuity of process* is affirmed by the scoffer within the church of whom Peter spoke (2 Peter 3:1-7). The whole point of Scripture is the declaration of the *divine acts* as alone creative and redemptive as against man's historical processes and his conceptions of religious and natural process. In Genesis alone, the *acts* include creation, the curse and penalty of the Fall on all creation, interposition in the affairs of Cain and Abel, Enoch, Noah and the flood, the call and blessing of Abraham, the judgment on Sodom and Gomorrah, and much more. To reduce creation to process means to naturalize all the rest of Scripture, step by step, if logic prevail, and it is significant to note the hostility of all believers in process to any attempt such as that by Whitcomb and Morris, in *The Genesis Flood* (1961), to give serious consideration to the Biblical narrative.

The ordination of believers in process is inconsistent with and contrary to the survival of orthodoxy, for process is inevitably a substitute decree for the eternal counsel of the triune God. It is in *radical* disagreement with the plain statement of Scripture, which is echoed in the Westminster Confession of Faith (chapt. IV) and the Larger Catechism (Q. 15). To affirm the *act* of creation is to affirm the sovereignty of God and the reality and priority of the eternal decree. No small stake is at issue in this controversy. In every affirmation of process, the sovereign and transcendent God is slowly and steadily enveloped in by the mists of immanence in man's beclouded mind, and He begins to disappear into a continuous ocean of being in process. Against this we must affirm that "The work of creation is that wherein God did in the beginning, by the word of his power, make of nothing the world and all things therein for himself, within the space of six days, and all very good" (The Larger Catechism, A. 15).

Chapter Eight

The Concept
of a Mature Creation

It has often been pointed out, frequently by scientists themselves, that much of the difference between ancient and contemporary science must be ascribed to the toolmaker who stands between, men like Anton van Leeuwenhoek, who made possible a wider range of observation and activity. This fact leads to two very apparent conclusions. First, much of what man popularly ascribes to the theorist, as he marvels at the results of science, properly belongs to the neglected toolmaker. Second, while the results of modern theoretical science are often valid and acceptable from the Biblical perspective, their validity no more guarantees the framework of secular scientific opinion than did the validity of much of Babylonian science underwrite Babylonian cosmology and scientific theory. In utilizing tools of various kinds as fashioned by diverse cultures, we are not thereby compelled to adopt those cultures. The fact that we use the Canaanite alphabet (for the Phoenicians were Canaanites) does not require us to do them honor.[1]

---

[1] Such honor, however, is often accorded them. See W. F. Albright, "The Role of the Canaanites in the History of Civilization," in G. Ernest Wright, ed., *The Bible and the Ancient Near East*, Essays in Honor of William Fox Albright (Garden City, N. Y.: Doubleday, 1961), 328-366.

Baal worship upheld, and was a religious expression of, *the concept of reality as process.* The religious faiths of ancient Europe, the Far East, the Near East, and North Africa represented variations of a common myth, the Python concept of chaos and cosmos and the history of creation "as a process of bringing order out of chaos."[2] Primitive American mythology cannot be definitely identified as derivative of the Python myth, but it does have "surprising correspondences."[3] While their relationship to the Python myth is questionable, the myths of the Americas are still clearly instances of faith in reality as process.

Similarly, modern science has, according to Hoagland and Bryson, "one principle" which undergirds all its thinking about reality. As Bryson stated it, "This is the principle, or the intellectual habit, of thinking of all reality as process." The modern biologist goes further. "Life is a process, yes. But man himself is a process." His body "is itself a process" and an exemplification of the principle of "ancient Heraclitus who said, 'all things flow.'"[4] Heraclitus deified process. For him, being is a perpetual becoming, a continual about-to-be, so that the only unchanging thing is change. The implications of this position, clearly apparent in modern thought, are relativistic. All things are relative save process, and everything in man or his society is related to or made one with process. Thus, for Bryson, man's morals and customs are *alike* "accidents of his time and place" and aspects of process.[5] Accordingly, "The modern social scientist is unlikely to see much good purpose in the magnificent abstractions of Good and Evil."[6] Indeed, man may "be on his way toward creating a new human species."[7] This is not a surprising conclusion or concern.

---

[2] Joseph Fontenrose, *Python, A Study of Delphic Myth and Its Origins* (Berkeley: University of California Press, 1959), 218, see 473.

[3] *Ibid.*, 505.

[4] Lyman Bryson, ed., *An Outline of Man's Knowledge of the Modern World* (Garden City, N.Y.: Doubleday, 1960), 141.

[5] *Ibid.*, 74.

[6] Meyer Maskin, M.D., "The Science of Personality," in Bryson, 117. Maskin a practicing psychiatrist and psychoanalyst, is Assistant Clinical Professor of Psychiatry at the New York University College of Medicine.

Wherever there is faith in reality as process, man's problem is not *ethical* but *metaphysical*, *not sin but finitude*. The philosopher and theologian of process will seek to deify man or his society in order to transcend finitude. The scientist will seek to surpass man by recreating him as a god in process. The physicist Joseph Harold Rush, for example, believed that man would learn to control "life processes," "biology of his own species," and perhaps ultimately, having conquered both space and death, endlessly explore the universe.[8] The whole point of the temptation in Genesis 3 was the insistence precisely that God's purpose in barring the tree of knowledge of good and evil was not *ethical* but *metaphysical*, not to keep man from sin but to keep him from being "as God" (Revised Version). The insistence of autonomous man's mythology and science is that reality is in process, and that the essence of this process is not ethical but cosmological, and in that sense metaphysical. Since his epistemology is apostate, to deny that reality is in process, biological and cosmological, is for him to deny the *possibility* of knowledge. According to Hoagland, "(George) Wald points out that there are only two answers to the question of how life began. It must either have arisen spontaneously from nonliving material or have been created by supernatural means. If one accepts the second answer, science has nothing to contribute, since the question cannot be resolved by the operational approaches of scientists."[9]

And if science has nothing to contribute, then the matter is settled against creation by the *a priori* assumptions of autonomous man. Questions which "cannot be resolved by the operational approaches of scientists" are considered by their very nature impossible in terms of this anthropocentric view. *Revelation must be ruled inadmissible precisely because it is revelation and hence beyond man*, who is creation's autonomous king and vanguard in the unfolding of process,

---

[7.] Maskin, *Ibid.*, in Bryson, 99.
[8.] J. H. Rush, *The Dawn of Life*, 236, 243-248; see especially J. H. Rush, "The Next 10,000 Years," *Saturday Review*, vol. XLI, no. 4 (25 January 1958):11-13, 36.
[9.] Hudson Hoagland, "The Elements of Life," in Bryson, 151.

and is now potentially able, it is held, to guide this process in his own case, and even to create new beings to be his servants, which will surpass God's handiwork, for "When man synthesizes his own versions of biological systems, he will have the advantage of design, of intelligent forethought."[10]

The conflict between Biblical religion and the science of autonomous man is real, necessary, and irreconcilable. Attention has been called to this conflict by Dr. Huston Smith, a professor of philosophy at Massachusetts Institute of Technology, in speaking "of the program on which science has embarked":

> This program has four parts, he said. First, creation of life, which he said has almost been achieved already. Second, creation of minds, as evidenced by the analogy between the mind and thinking-machines presently being pressed to the hilt. Third, creation of adjusted individuals via drugs, tranquilizers and other chemistry. And fourth, creation of a good society via "behavioral engineering," subliminal or otherwise.
>
> "I personally don't see how this four-fold program can be squared with religion," Dr. Smith said. "To the extent that it (the program) is taken seriously, God is dead: to the extent that it becomes validated, God will be buried. Far from being a thing of the past, the conflict between science and religion may be shaping up in proportions greater than any we have thus far known."[11]

Against all this, the implications of the Biblical position are clear-cut, and its declarations sharply challenging.

In spite of every effort to allegorize Genesis 1, the meaning is textually clear: a six-day creative work by God is asserted. Every attempt to adopt the framework hypothesis and invalidate the six days proves too much: similar frameworks and patterns can be and have been read into the accounts of the virgin birth and the resurrection to undercut their meaning.[12] As Marcus Dods stated it, "If, for example, the word 'day' in

---

10. Rush, *Saturday Review, loc. cit.*
11. "Conflict of Science, Religion, Seen Increasing," *The Presbyterian Journal*, vol. XIX, no. 45, (8 March 1961): 3.

these chapters, does not mean a period of twenty-four hours, the interpretation of Scripture is hopeless."[13]

Another common mode of misinterpreting Genesis 1 has been the attempt to translate Genesis 1:1 and part of verses 2 and 3 as a dependent clause.[14] "Absolute creation" is ruled out by this construction, and "pre-existing matter" is placed side by side with God as the *Given*. This interpretation, as Young has pointed out, is also untenable.[15]

Genesis 1 is perfectly clear in its declaration of a *mature creation* in six days. This cannot be ruled out as a "poetic narrative" without violence to the plain intent of Scripture and a consequent Barthian separation between faith and history. Genesis 1 mandates certain requirements for both science and religion which cannot be avoided. *Basic* to these requirements is the concept of a physically and biologically *mature creation*. This, even for evolutionists, is in a sense an inescapable concept, in that, where a mature creation is denied, a mature potentiality must be asserted, a potentiality in the first atom as mature as the potentiality of an infinite universe in its infinite future. As Boardman long ago stated it, in order to vindicate creative evolution:

> Suppose you say it came from a few cells or germs, or perhaps one. That does not answer the question. The axiom, "Every effect must have a cause," implies another axiom, "Effects are proportional to their causes"—that is to say, causes are measured by their effects. If the whole

---

[12.] For the six days, see L. Berkhof: *Systematic Theology* (Grand Rapids: Eerdmans, 1946), 150-164. See also R. F. Surburg, "In the Beginning God Created," in Paul A. Zimmerman, *Darwin, Evolution, and Creation*, 57-64, (St. Louis: Concordia, 1959), 57-64. Again see Henry M. Morris and John C. Whitcomb, Jr., *The Genesis Flood* (Philadelphia: Presbyterian and Reformed, 1961).

[13.] Marcus Dods, *The Book of Genesis* (New York: Armstrong, 1907), 4. In making this statement, Dods was not trying to defend the orthodox position, since he believed in evolution, but to insist on honest exegesis.

[14.] It is so translated, for example, in Smith and Goodspeeds translation, *The Complete Bible, An American Translation*, (Chicago: The University of Chicago Press), 1939, and also by Theodore H. Robinson, *The Book of Genesis* (London: National Adult School Union).

[15.] Edward J. Young, "The Relation of the First Verse of Genesis to Verses Two and Three," *The Westminster Theological Journal*, vol. XXI, no. 2 (May 1959): 133-146.

material universe came from a few germs and *from nothing else*, then the weight of these germs must be equal to the weight of the universe. You cannot get out of a thing more than is in it. It is a maxim of philosophy: "Evolution implies previous involution." And the axiom that every effect must have an adequate cause demands that the involution must be equal to the evolution. You cannot evolve what was not involved.[16]

The answer of the contemporary scientist is to deny all such "laws" *in argument* while operating in terms of them *in research*. The essential point, however, is this: a philosophy of process asserts a mature potentiality in man and creation; a Biblical philosophy asserts a mature creation.

The difference in perspective now becomes apparent. A *mature potentiality* means that man's present problem is finitude. A *mature creation* means that man's problem is ethical, is sin. In terms of a mature creation, process exists, but it is not biological process from amoeba to man and man to superman, but biological decay and death. Historically, process is the development of man in terms of his implications, in terms of ethical and epistemological self-consciousness. Man is not moving from non-being into being, nor is his a perpetual becoming. He is a creature created in the image of God, moving either in terms of making his fall or his creation-image explicit. Culturally, he develops either the implications of his apostasy into the total solipsism of autonomy from God, or, in terms of the image of God, man becomes king over creation and its priest and prophet under God.

Moreover, in a mature creation, the standard is a creation wholly good as well as mature, so that the normal is not the statistical average, i.e., sickly and diseased in the main, but the new creation in Jesus Christ. With reference to man specifically, the mature man as created in Adam and re-created in Jesus Christ is the standard. Since man was created full-grown and mature, this maturity is normative in his biology

---

[16.] George D. Boardman, *Studies in the Creative Week* (New York: Apple-ton, 1878), 39.

and in his psychology. In an evolving creation, the "germ" with its potential is the law and the standard, so that what Van Til has called integration into the void prevails.[17] Thus, for Freud, childhood and the unconscious are determinative of man, in that the child and the preconscious existence of man are more basic and original than the mature man, a late-comer on the scene. Thus, Ralph Waldo Gerard, M.D., Director of Laboratories at the University of Michigan's Mental Research Institute, can assert that "the sleeping rather than the waking state seems to be the more primitive and the preferred one."[18] From the Biblical perspective, any such preference is sin, and man's infantilism is rebellion against his being, which is to be a mature man in God's image. Man is not struggling towards this maturity but is in flight from it. He has not struggled to consciousness but is in war against it and in flight from it because it thunders with demands that he be a responsible and mature man under God. Biblical process is therefore in terms of the development of the responsibilities of the mature creature or the development of the implications of the headlong flight from that maturity.

The concept of evolutionary process is by its adherents used in a double sense with reference to man: to demean man and yet to exalt him. As against the ethical Biblical doctrine of man as created in God's image and responsible to Him, there is a studied reduction of man to meaninglessness. His mind, we are told, is nothing but a mechanism, and man an animal. Mind may indeed be ultimately determined to have been no more than "a sort of phylogenetic tumor" which leads to man's self-destruction, we are warned. "Evolution is creative, but its creativity is independent of purpose or design. It is a result of the properties of interacting atoms and molecules."[19] Mind can thus be viewed as the property of man's nervous system, even as "magnetism is a property of the structure and organization

---

[17.] See C. Van Til, *Psychology of Religion*, 1935, and R. J. Rushdoony, *By What Standard?* (Vallecito, Calif.: Ross House Books, 1959), 65-80.
[18.] Gerard, "The Brain: Mechanism of the Mind," in Bryson, 83.
[19.] Hoagland, 59-161.

of iron atoms." Thus, man, created in the image of God, is reduced to a mechanism "probably descended from the chance organization of a few giant molecules." Then, surprisingly, we are told, "But this in no way need militate against the significance and dignity of human life as it has emerged from both biological and social evolution. Men's highly developed cerebral cortex has produced remarkable intellectual achievements."[20] This paradox stems from the two concepts of ultimacy employed by evolutionists. First, the molecules or atoms are prior and hence more ultimate aspects of reality. As a result, the Biblical concept of mature man can be riddled with the claims of molecules and the vast ocean of unconsciousness. Man therefore cannot be the man God requires him to be. His physical impulses are more ultimate than any ethics he may have devised or received. The mature man, made "little less than heavenly beings" (Ps. 8:5, Berkeley Version), is instead made little lower than the ultimate and all-powerful molecules. Biblical faith, therefore, in its ethical mandate, is seen as hopelessly *unrealistic* in expecting man to conform to a law so alien to his being. This doctrine of ultimacy is used to undercut the covenant and to vindicate man as a covenant-breaker. It denies that man's problem is *ethical* in order to exalt him *metaphysically*.

This having been accomplished, a second concept of ultimacy is now brought into play. Process in this evolutionary mythology does indeed originate in molecules, and molecules are thus in a very real sense ultimate as against any God who may exist, and they are prior to any ethical and religious covenant that God may claim to be in force. This process, however, points always to a new ultimate in its continual becoming, and, since, as many hold, man is now rapidly becoming able to guide his own evolution, *man is thus the new ultimate in process*. As such, his position has indeed *metaphysical* "significance and dignity," because man now has no law outside of himself. He is both molecules, and therefore

---

20. *Ibid.*, 160.

free from the covenant by their priority, and also man, the (ostensibly) autonomous ultimate in process and the interpreter of being and becoming. He is both lawmaker and law, the developing interpretation and the interpreter.

As against this, we must assert the doctrine of the mature work of creation, the implications of which are thus stated by Van Til:

> If the creation doctrine is thus taken seriously, it follows that the various aspects of created reality must sustain such relations to one another as have been ordained between them by the Creator, as superiors, inferiors or equals. All aspects being equally created, no one aspect of reality may be regarded as more ultimate than another. Thus the created one and many may in this respect be said to be equal to one another; they are equally derived and equally dependent upon God who sustains them both. The particulars or facts of the universe do and must act in accord with universals or laws. Thus there is order in the created universe. On the other hand, the laws may not and can never reduce the particulars to abstract particulars or reduce their individuality in any manner. The laws are but generalizations of God's method of working with the particulars. God may at any time take one fact and set it into a new relation to created law. That is, there is no inherent reason in the facts or laws themselves why this should not be done. It is this sort of conception of the relation of facts and laws, of the temporal one and many, imbedded as it is in that idea of God in which we profess to believe, that we need in order to make room for miracles. And miracles are at the heart of the Christian position.[21]

The ultimacy of God is the issue in the concept of a mature creation.

[21.] Cornelius Van Til, *The Defense of the Faith* (Philadelphia: The Presbyterian and Reformed Publishing Co., 1955), 44.

Chapter Nine

Process and History

The revolt against the sovereign decree of the triune God is waged in the name of "rescuing" the validity of history from the predetermination of an eternal counsel. Inevitably, however, this attempt to give meaning to time from within time leads to the radical contempt of time and history. The Hellenic faith in process led to the Stoic resignation from history, and the Renaissance and Enlightenment, in giving priority to time over eternity, led to the existentialist terror of time. Time, when deified, turns out to be not divine but demonic.

It would be easy, of course, to document this by citing existentialist and neo-orthodox thinkers. For Karl Barth, for example, "God" is divorced from omnipotence and given the radical "freedom" of process: he can tomorrow be the reverse of himself, can be demonic, or whatever he will, as an aspect of his "freedom." Thus, no eternal decree is conceivable, and time is ostensibly rescued for man. But process and history are at the same time divorced from the realm of faith and meaning; indeed, for faith to depend on history as revelatory of an eternal decree is to "destroy" faith and the true decree, which is in terms of man's own inner process. Thus Barth "saves"

man not only from the God of Scripture and Calvin, but also
from time itself, and delivers him into the chaos of his own
dialectic as the ground of his new creation.

This same surrender of time and history can be seen very
clearly, and more naively, in Huston Smith, as he comments
on the bodily resurrection of Christ. He grants that "the
resurrection faith did not deal with the fate of a good man. Its
full referent was the character of God and the nature of
ultimate reality."[1] If it is "the nature of ultimate reality" which
is at issue, we would then assume that the bodily resurrection
must be insisted on, for otherwise we have no evidence of that
reality being victorious over death. But Smith assures us that
the bodily resurrection is not a necessity:

> Most Christians today continue to believe in the bodily
> resurrection of Christ, but even of those who do not, most
> claim to share in the resurrection faith. For if the ultimate
> referent of this faith is not what happened to a particular
> human frame but rather the status of God—his absolute
> lordship over both nature and history—"modernist"
> Christians claim to be in full accord with the original
> Christians on the central point in question.... But to insist
> that despite the scantiness of our evidence there is only
> one legitimate view as to what happened in nature and
> history that first Easter is to focus the resurrection faith on
> physical externals instead of on the central point.[2]

Thus, an insistence on the bodily resurrection as essential is to
miss "the central point." But what is this "central point"?
Smith has stated that it is "the status of God—his absolute
lordship over both nature and history." Yet, what "happened
in nature and history that first Easter" *cannot* be identified
with the bodily resurrection, i.e., with *the historical and natural
facts of the case!* It is clear, therefore, that Smith, in common
with neo-orthodoxy, has rejected the usual definition of God,
nature, and history. His "God" does not have to reveal himself
in nature and history to be real; his nature is distinct from this

---

[1] Huston Smith, *The Religions of Man* (New York: Mentor Books, 1959),
283.
[2] *Ibid.*, 284.

cosmos; and his history is independent of time and historical process. Indeed, after Kant, we must seek Smith's God, nature, history, time, and eternity in the determinative mind of autonomous man. This divorce from the God of Scripture, the ontological Trinity, is also a divorce from nature, time, and history. The overthrow of the eternal decree leaves man with a temporal decree that is anti-historical and is reduced to dependence on the processes of each particular mind, which leads to the total anarchy of these multiple absolutes.

A philosophy of biological process is therefore also a metaphysics which destroys historical process in favor of existentialist and dialectical processes. The mind of man, expressing itself in terms of "faith," becomes either the ground or else the manifestation of revelation, and is thus the voice and control of revelation. When the historicity of the first Adam is undercut, then the historicity of Christ—and the validity of all history—is also destroyed. Biological process as being-in-becoming cannot tolerate the interference in time of God, the absolute and uncreated being, nor can the new absolute in process of becoming, the autonomous mind of man, allow any reality in history, any "physical externals," to challenge its own autonomy or the priority of its becoming, which is the truly "central point."

Thus, modernists who began the century busily creating and fashioning their own "historical Jesus," i.e., a Jesus completely divorced from the eternal decree and made fully a child of process, soon turned their backs on their own idol, this "historical Jesus," in favor of "the Jesus of faith," in whom the divorce from eternity was followed by a divorce from time.

In philosophy the dignity of "clock time" has been supplanted by a new kind of time, "time lived," which, simultaneous with its exaltation, has become the focal point of man's sickness. In spite of this disease of time lived, man perversely sees his evil as epitomized in time by the clock. As Levi points out with reference to Gabriel Marcel's *The Philosophy of Existence*, "The time-table, the schedule, and the clock are here the symbols of man's alienation from an intrinsically human world."[3] From the Biblical perspective, the triumph of man under God involves the conquest of time and history, its redemption in terms of covenantal purpose, by timetable, schedule, and clock, among many other things. Man, seen in the perspective of "God's eternal decree," is, according to chapter three of the Westminster Confession of Faith, free when predetermined. The predestination of "whatsoever comes to pass" by God is the very ground of man's liberty, for "the liberty or contingency of second causes" is not "taken away, but rather established," by the eternal decree. This concept undergirded the exuberant conquest of time and nature by Western man as scientist. The world of the clock, timetable, and schedule was seen as the liberation of man in terms of his purposive mastery of time and nature. But, as scientific man moved steadily away from his Christian origin and perspective into a philosophy of process, he perversely saw the timetable, clock and schedule as, first, a means of dehumanizing man as against God's insistence that man is primarily covenant man, and, second, as a tyrant to be rebelled against in the name of freedom. Thus, at the moment of science's triumph, science began to be viewed as demonic by its very own sons, who sought vain refuge from the clock of history in "time lived." Levi has cited "the narcissistic subjectivity of all philosophy since the Renaissance: that whether it begins at the beginning, the middle, or the end, it always takes as its point of departure the epistemic properties of the human self."[4] In literature, the keynote of Proust's thinking is "Everything mysteriously pointing to the experiences of a self lost somewhere in the labyrinth of Time."[5] Time, which was to have been autonomous man's defense against eternity, has become a juggernaut relentlessly destroying man's lonely self. And no wonder: time being subordinate to the sovereign decree of God in eternity, it can

---

3. Albert William Levi, *Philosophy and the Modern World* (Bloomington: Indiana University Press, 1959), 18.
4. *Ibid.*, 64.
5. *Ibid.*, 73.

only serve Him who created it and can only have meaning in terms of His eternal counsel.

There is another aspect to the flight from time and the contempt of history. According to "the interpretive results of the newer physics.... The concept of time with its order of before and after derives from the notion of causality. There is no absolute simultaneity because the speed of light is finite; that is, causal transmission requires time."[6] Man, being in rebellion against law and causality as infringements on his *becoming* and on his ultimacy in process, must therefore be also in rebellion against clock time as the epitome of his slavery. Clock time is a bondage whose ticking always and monotonously moves in terms of an eternal decree external to and transcending man. Man's rebellion against eternity must therefore be followed by a rebellion against time. Time always beats to and echoes the stroke of eternity. When Augustine broke away from "the Greek Idea of time," he paved the way "for an authentic ground-motive."[7] Even this small hint of the implications of time has been sufficient to haunt Western man with the spectre of eternity. Time refuses to have reference to itself alone, and it is manifestly impossible for the mind of man to comprehend and control it by his own decree.

> The modal diversity of meaning exists only in the coherence of all modal aspects, but it is the expression of a totality of signification which through the medium of time is broken up into a modal diversity of aspects.

> The totality or fulness of meaning is the necessary transcendent centre where, in their mutual coherence, all modal aspects converge into *the unity of direction towards the Origin, towards the* arche *of all meaning.*[8]

Thus the rejection of God inevitably requires as its logical concomitant the rejection of time. Man seeks either to arrest time by his own decree, as from the days of the Tower of Babel

---

6. *Ibid.*, 268.
7. Herman Dooyeweerd, *A New Critique of Theoretical Thought*, vol. I (Philadelphia: Presbyterian and Reformed, 1953), 179.
8. *Ibid.*, 16.

to Hitler's "thousand year" Reich and the United Nations, or to flee from time by the clock, from history into *mysticism,* time lived. In either case, man as god is saying, "Time shall be no more."

Man is thus a temporal creature in rebellion against time and hence against his own being. Because he sees his problem as not ethical but metaphysical, time is, in terms of his philosophy of process, a disease in man to be overcome. Man's *becoming* is thus a process of overcoming the limitations of death, time, and history. It is no wonder, then, that the historical and bodily resurrection of Jesus Christ is an offense to modern man. After all, his own temporal and bodily existence is increasingly also an offense to him because he refuses to be a creature and strives in his heart "to be as God."

Chapter Ten

Science and Decree

We have seen that, as Huston Smith has pointed out, science has embarked on a fourfold program whereby life, mind, man, and society are to be created or recreated by a science which displaces God as the source of the eternal decree. Smith, of course, has a happy solution to this conflict of science and religion. He sees a "revolution in Western thought" producing "a new view of reality" which is bringing science, philosophy, and religion together in a common allegiance to process![1]

We must bypass this happy return to Baalism for a further consideration of the fourfold program. It is in essence a new sovereign decree. Thus, it is not predestination in itself which is an offense to man, but predestination *by God*. The culmination of process is control of the various aspects and phases of process by scientific man, so that evolution is to be guided and controlled, life is to be created, minds invented as tools of the new gods, human minds shaped and directed by the gods of science through chemistry, and society itself made into a great machine in which man, economics, education, sexual reproduction, and all else are made subservient to

---

[1.] See Huston Smith, "The Revolution in Western Thought," *The Saturday Evening Post*, vol. 234, no. 34, 26 August 1961, 28-29, 59-60.

predestination by scientific controllers. This form of predestination is the truly horrible decree.

This new doctrine of predestination rests, moreover, on a background of universal mindlessness and chance. The vast ocean of being-in-process has been guided by no mind and has operated in terms of chance set in the context of endless and infinite process. The "god" of this vast ocean is *time*, for, given enough time, it is believed that all miracles are possible and even certain. Bryson has stated it more strongly:

> The laws of chance do not entirely eliminate even the remotest possibility. If the earth is at least 5,000 million years old, almost anything, however unlikely, could have happened here at least once; and it needed to happen only once.[2]

Handrich, in discussing radioactivity as an age-indicator, has pointed out how the evidence militates against these vast time schemes.[3] For religious reasons, however, such an argument is ineffectual with most scientists, whose faith requires the long time-spans to account for miracles which are clearly contrary to all contemporary scientific theory. Hoagland has clearly stated what it is believed that chance and time can do:

> But a special view of probability is required when one thinks about these matters. According to this view, if an extremely improbable event needs to occur but *once*, then the likelihood of its occurrence becomes increasingly possible the longer time permitted for a variety of trials. In the case of possible spontaneous generation from life, as we shall see, there have been a great many opportunities for chance to bring all sorts of molecules together over an exceedingly long time.
>
> ...But Wald has also pointed out how highly improbable events (if they occur but once, or only rarely) may become highly probable given a long enough time and enough trials. Spontaneous generation is such a once-to-happen variety of phenomena, since once a primitive organism

---

[2] Bryson, 139.
[3] Theodore L. Handrich, *The Creation, Facts, Theories and Faith* (Chicago: The Moody Press, 1953), 239-260.

that can reproduce itself is formed, natural selection could modify it and start life on its way down the ages.

Wald gives several illustrations of this point about probability. For example, the chance that a coin when tossed will not fall head up in a single toss is one half. The chance that no head will appear in a series of ten tosses is one half multiplied by itself ten times, that is $(1/2)^{10}$ or one in a thousand. Therefore, the chance that a head will appear at least once in ten trials is 999/1,000 or a virtual certainty. Let us consider the example of an event which has a chance of happening only once in a thousand times. The chance that such an event will not occur in any one try is 99 out of 1,000. However, in 1,000 trials, this chance becomes 999/1,000 multiplied by itself 1,000 times, and this turns out to be 37/1,000. The chance that it will happen at least once is therefore 63/100 or better than 3 out of 5. In 10,000 trials the chance that this event will occur at least once is 19,999/20,000—a virtual certainty. Thus very improbable events may become highly probable ones, given enough time and trials.[4]

This illustration is of course a variation of the earlier and more familiar one: if a hundred monkeys at a hundred typewriters typed for enough millennia, they would through sheer chance reproduce *all* the plays of Shakespeare. The sorry fact about both illustrations is a very obvious oversight. Where did the hundred monkeys, typewriters, paper, coins, and tosser come from first of all? Who is to keep the tosser tossing, the coins from wear or loss, the monkeys from wrecking the typewriters in the first try, and so on? *To account for the potentialities of chance, a vast realm of being and purposive activity must first be presupposed.* What is called the operation of chance more closely resembles controlled experimentation in a laboratory. Controlled possibility in terms of necessary and provided materials is by no means to be confused with chance. Thus, the concept of chance which is employed is a self-contradictory concept and is by no means valid at any point.

[4.] Hoagland, in Bryson, 152 f.

Despite this confusion, the fact remains that the scientist *believes* in chance as the agent of cosmic catalysis, as the god which fathered the universe and man. Now, however, the old god is in triumphant process of being unseated by the new gods, the scientists, whose intelligent eternal decree or control will steadily become the new source of creation. Thus, even as Uranus was castrated by Cronus in Greek mythology, so chance is being steadily eliminated by scientific controls designed to govern the total life and economy of man in terms of the new eternal decree of science. Those who welcome this new society forget that Cronus maintained his decree only so long as he devoured his children.

A cosmos, or a society, fashioned and controlled by man will inevitably serve man's purposes. A society controlled by scientists will only serve the radically relativistic purposes of the new gods and none other. As the new philosopher-kings and platonic guardians, they will assume the role of God, mind and purpose for society, as a living source of the counsel of predestination.

A world created by God will inevitably serve God's purposes because it is governed by His sovereign decree. In terms of this, creation cannot serve the fourfold program of scientists nor be amenable to it, inasmuch as it is beyond their control and impervious to their reckoning. God, who created all things out of nothing, so that not only the universe but also "space" itself came into being by His sovereign decree, alone governs that creation and alone established its nature and destiny. "The people imagine a vain thing" (Ps. 2:1) when they take counsel together concerning their pretensions, hopes, and programs.

The philosophy of process, as it appears in churchmen, is responsible for a double heresy: first, process or works is introduced into the order of salvation to diminish or supplant the saving work of God with man's own efficacious act. Second, process or works is introduced into the creation of the universe in order to diminish or set aside the divine act, and, behind it, the divine decree, in favor of a new, emergent, and increasingly decisive decree, the sovereign work of scientific man.

The fourfold program poses no metaphysical threat to the faith; it does pose an ethical threat to all men in the form of God's judgment. As Donald Cowan has observed, "The completely secular ideology of the modern scientist is reflected in the total relativism of our dominant cosmological myth.... Our modern cosmological myths are devoid of moral and spiritual content."[5]

The absence of this content is a philosophical necessity. Just as law cannot be set above God without becoming a god over God, so a moral law cannot be set above scientific man without infringing upon his sovereignty. It is significant that increasingly "scientific" educators, after Dewey, refuse to hope for a "changed" society and speak rather of the goal of a "changing" or controlled society, always fully controlled and always in process for process' sake. The radical "freedom" from all law save process leaves this new god-man free to reign in a hell and chaos of his own designing.

This "freedom" the fallen sons of Adam have sought since their banishment from Eden. Darwin therefore met, not a scientific need, but a religious hunger. When his *On the Origin of Species by Means of Natural Selection* was published on November 24, 1859, the entire edition of 1,250 copies sold out on the day of publication: its contents met with a fanatical popular approval before a word of it had been read! Men have been pleased to invent a myth of the persecution of this new idea. In reality, the opposition was scattered, and came more from some scientists than churchmen, scientists in the exact sciences who were shocked at the substitution of theory for observation. Bernard Shaw, in commenting on the happy reception the theory of evolution received, remarked, "If you can realize how insufferably the world was oppressed by the notion that everything that happened was an arbitrary

---

5. Donald Cowan, "Modern Creation Myth," *National Review*, vol. XI, no.8, 26 August 1961, 128 f.

personal act of an arbitrary personal God of dangerous, jealous and cruel personal character, you will understand how the world jumped at Darwin."[6] Lunn, in citing Darwin's success, observed, "his immense success was partly due to the fact that he happened to restate these theories at the precise moment when theophobia (the fear or dislike of God) was on the increase, and when a majority of scientists were looking for some alternative to what Husley calls 'the untenable theory of special creation.'"[7]

Thus the rebellion is against the eternal decree of God in favor of the new and sovereign decree of scientific man. The controversy between contemporary science and Biblical faith is not a scientific issue, but a religious one, and some scientists are becoming aware of this fact. This is clearly apparent in an article by a biochemist, Philip Siekewitz, in *The Nation*, September 3, 1958:

> The revolution going on in the biological sciences, mainly in biochemistry, will make atomic energy look like child's play.... Therefore, and more urgently than ever, we need a revolution in our political and social institutions to cope with these findings.... We are even about to learn how to change ourselves.... I think that we are approaching the greatest event in human history, even in the history of life on this earth, and that is the deliberate changing by man of many of the biological processes.... With all the knowledge thus gained, we will be able to plan ahead so that our children will be what we would like them to be— physically and even mentally. At this point, man will be remolding his own being. Theologians will protest but it is certainty itself that man will play God.

Here is rampant pride that the scientist will outdo God and usher in "the greatest event in human history." Because of this scientific man who is insistent on "playing God," we are asked to alter "our political and social institutions" in terms of the

---

6. Cited by Arnold Lunn, ed. of Douglas Dewar and H. S. Shelton, *Is Evolution Proved? A Debate* (London: Hollis and Carter, 1947), 4.
7. *Ibid.*, 4.

reality of this new "god." It is no wonder that Edmund A. Opitz, in citing these words, observes:

> This may not be madness, but surely it approaches the brink of madness of a sort. In any event, those who resist the idea of both the molding and the being remolded had better retrace their steps to the point where our path took a wrong turning. The recovery of sanity will be a route different from the one we have been following.[8]

8. Edmund A. Opitz, *Despotism by Consent* (Irvington-on-Hudson, N.Y.: Foundation for Economic Education, 1961), 8.

Chapter Eleven

Paradigms and Facts

Louis Leakey, director of Kenya's Centre for Prehistory and Palaeontology in Nairobi, described his discovery, together with his wife Mary, of a bit of skull and two teeth, in these words: "We knelt together to examine the treasure...and almost cried with sheer joy. For years people had been telling us that we'd better stop looking, but I felt deep down that it had to be there. You must be patient about these things." The time was July 17, 1959.[1] This scene is a curious one on two counts. *First*, the scientist Leakey knew what he had found before he had examined it: he worked by faith, and viewed his findings by faith. He was finding "proof" for a theory already accepted, and he accepted his finding as "proof" on sight. *Second*, the intense emotionalism and joy sound more like a revival experience than a scientific analysis.

In the same article, author Pfeiffer, himself a true believer in evolution, reports on the intense emotionalism of evolutionists:

[1.] John Pfeiffer, "Man—Through Time's Mists," *The Saturday Evening Post*, 239th year, no. 25, 3 December 1966, 41.

111

Among those leading the current research boom are adventurers, men with strong personalities and a willingness to spend their lives following up leads and hunches. This spirit apparently goes with strong emotions, and feelings often run high when it comes to interpreting evidence. Criticism is sometimes regarded, and perhaps intended, as a deep personal insult.

Not long ago a professor wrote an article questioning a former teacher, in the mildest possible terms, about the authenticity of a certain find—and ended a friendship of 30 years. On another occasion an eminent anthropologist arose to speak at a meeting given in his honor, and began reminiscing about the early days of his career when his ideas concerning human evolution had been ignored. But he managed to complete only a few sentences of his talk. Then, overcome by the recollection of years of frustration, he lowered his head and burst into tears. Investigators have stalked out of meetings, indulged in personal vituperation (in technical journals as well as privately), argued over priorities, accused colleagues of stealing their ideas.

Such behavior may be somewhat less common than it once was, and it is by no means unknown in other areas of science, but its incidence has been strikingly high among pre-historians. The reason for this occupational ailment is obscure, but it may have something to do with the shortage of solid evidence.[2]

It is well to have this fact admitted by the evolutionists themselves. Creationists have long known the savage and intemperate emotionalism with which evolutionists respond to criticism of their conclusions, or even to critical questioning. Such responses are scarcely the popular image of what passes for science, but they do remain the reality of modern science. "Its incidence has been strikingly high" among evolutionists, we are told, and with reason. No area of intellectual or scientific study can dispense with reasoning, but very few areas are ready to face up to the fact that all reasoning is circular reasoning. In many areas, there is general agreement about the particular form of circularity, and hence some

---

2. *Ibid.*, 42.

general peace to the same degree. In evolutionary studies, where agreement is less general, there is as a result extensive conflict.

To understand this problem, it is necessary to examine the nature of thought. All thinking rests on pre-theoretical presuppositions, in essence religious commitments, which condition the nature of thinking. These pre-theoretical presuppositions determine which experiences out of all man's sense impressions shall be regarded as *facts*. Thus, before there are facts, there are already *presuppositions*, which lead to various *beliefs and theories*, which determine what shall be regarded as *factuality*. In other words, before there is a fact, there is a faith about facts. As Cornelius Van Til has said, "facts and interpretations of facts cannot be separated. It is impossible even to discuss any particular fact except in relation to some universal. The real question about facts is, therefore, what kind of universal can give the best account of the facts. Or rather, the real question is which universal can state or give meaning to any fact."[3] There is thus no such thing as uninterpreted factuality. Van Til continues:

> ...it is impossible to reason on the basis of brute facts. Everyone who reasons about facts comes to those facts with a schematism into which he fits the facts. The real question is, therefore, into whose schematism the facts will fit. As between Christianity and its opponents the question is whether our claim that Christianity is the only schematism into which the facts will fit, is truth or not. Christianity claims that unless we pre-suppose the existence of God, in whom, as the self-sufficient One, schematism and fact, fact and reason apart from and prior to the existence of the world, are coterminous, we face the utterly unintelligible "brute fact."[4]

To believe that "brute facts" can add up to knowledge is to believe that zeros can add up to something more than zero.[5]

[3.] Cornelius Van Til, *Christian — Theistic Evidences*, syllabus (Westminster Theological Seminary: Philadelphia, 1947), i ff.
[4.] *Ibid.*, 39.
[5.] *Ibid.*, 76.

The success of modern science has been due to its "borrowed capital," because modern science is like the prodigal son. He left his father's house and is rich, but the substance he expends is his father's wealth.[6] In 1939, Van Til wrote:

> Thus the first step that the current scientific method is asking you to take is to assume that the facts that you meet are brute, that is, uninterpreted facts. *I say you are asked to assume the existence of brute facts.* If you did not assume this you could not be neutral with respect to various interpretations given of the facts. *If God exists there are no brute facts;* if God exists our study of facts must be the effort to know them as God wants them to be known by us. We must then seek to think God's thoughts after him. To assume that there are brute facts is therefore to assume that God does not exist.[7]

But, in recent years, the older scientific attitude has been giving way to something that seems to be a recognition of Van Til's position. A physicist whose thinking is becoming very influential concedes the circularity of scientific thinking. According to Thomas S. Kuhn, scientific thinking rests on "paradigms," on "universally recognized scientific achievements that for a time provide model problems and solutions to a community of practitioners."[8] The term "paradigms," he adds, "relates closely to 'normal science.'"[9] The paradigm is a body of presuppositions which make science possible. "No natural history can be interpreted in the absence of at least some implicit body of intertwined theoretical and methodological belief that permits selection, evaluation, and criticism."[10] Without these presuppositions, all data are equally relevant and equally meaningless. "In the absence of a paradigm or some candidate for a paradigm, all the facts that

---

[6.] *Ibid.*, 77.

[7.] Cornelius Van Til, "A Calvin University," *The Banner*, November 1939.

[8.] Thomas S. Kuhn, *The Structure of Scientific Revolutions* (Chicago: University of Chicago Press, Phoenix Books, 1964), x. Also issued as vol. II, no. 2, of the *International Encyclopedia of Unified Science* (University of Chicago Press, 1962).

[9.] *Ibid.*, 10.

[10.] *Ibid.*, 16 f.

could possibly pertain to the development of a given science are likely to seem equally relevant."[11] A paradigm is an accepted model or pattern which establishes what shall be regarded as science. It defines both the problems of science and the area of the answers.[12] The paradigm refuses to tolerate data which do not conform to the presuppositions:

> Mopping-up operations are what engage most scientists throughout their careers. They constitute what I am here calling normal science. Closely examined, whether historically or in the contemporary laboratory, that enterprise seems an attempt to force nature into the preformed and relatively inflexible box that the paradigm supplies. No part of the aim of normal science is to call forth new sorts of phenomena; indeed those that will not fit the box are often not seen at all. Nor do scientists normally aim to invent new theories, and they are often intolerant of those invented by others. Instead, normal scientific research is directed to the articulation of those phenomena and theories that the paradigm already supplies.
>
> Perhaps these are defects. The areas investigated by normal science are, of course, minuscule; the enterprise now under discussion has drastically restricted vision. But those restrictions, born from confidence in a paradigm, turn out to be essential to the development of science. By focusing attention upon a small range of relatively esoteric problems, the paradigm forces scientists to investigate some part of nature in a detail and depth that would otherwise be unimaginable.[13]

A paradigm is thus "a criterion for choosing problems." Other problems are dismissed as "metaphysical," although they may have been relevant previously. Science, Kuhn says, progresses rapidly because it chooses only those problems it can solve in terms of its paradigm. The paradigm will actually "insulate the community from those socially important problems that are not reducible to the puzzle form," that is, to the form required

---

11. *Ibid.*, 15.
12. *Ibid.*, 23 f.
13. *Ibid.*, 24.

for solution by the paradigm. There is no science without commitment to a paradigm. Kuhn speaks "of the paradigm-embodied experience of the race."[14] Man operates in every area in terms of basic presuppositions, and these presuppositions tell him what reality is.

Returning to science, Kuhn points out that circular reasoning is used to defend the basic presuppositions. In times of change, "Each group uses its own paradigm to argue in that paradigm's defense," with a "resulting circularity." "The circular argument...cannot be made logically or even probabilistically compelling for those who refuse to step into the circle." In times of change, a paradigm is stretched to the point where a somewhat new one begins to take over; the "two scientific schools disagree about what is a problem and what is a solution." Paradigms have a priority in all scientific work. Paradigms change only with crises, with a scientific revolution. The reasons for the change "do not derive from the logical structure of scientific knowledge." When the paradigm shifts, there is also a shift in what constitutes a problem and where the solution can be found.[15]

Paradigms "are constitutive of science," but there is "a sense in which they are constitutive of nature as well." Does this mean that there is an ultimate decree of God which can be discerned in all of nature? This Kuhn will not even consider. His own paradigm does not permit it. For him, each scientific revolution, or change of paradigm, is a change of world view. In this sense, "when paradigms change, the world itself changes with them."[16] Kuhn is not returning to a pre-Kantian belief in an objective world, tempting though that world is. He is clearly a post-Kantian humanist, a scientist who wants science without conceding reality to the world with which science is concerned. The measurements of science are not "the given" of experience but "the collected with difficulty," and laboratory

---

14. *Ibid.*, 37, 99, 127.
15. *Ibid.*, 43-52, 93-94, 108.
16. *Ibid.*, 109-110.

operations and measurements are, he admits, "paradigm—predetermined." What is their relation to the "real" world?

> But is sensory experience fixed and neutral? Are theories simply man-made interpretations of given data? The epistemological viewpoint that has most often guided Western philosophy for three centuries dictates an immediate and unequivocal, Yes! In the absence of derived alternatives, I find it impossible to relinquish entirely that viewpoint. Yet it no longer functions effectively, and the attempts to make it do so through the introduction of a neutral language of observations now seem to me hopeless.[17]

The sensory experience is itself paradigm-determined as well as the interpretation. Thus "fact" as well as "theory" are products of the paradigm, the presupposition. Hence the thorough circularity of reasoning. Hence the reason "why the proponents of competing paradigms must fail to make complete contact with each other's viewpoints." Paradigms so govern science that all past science is reviewed and seen in terms of progress towards the present paradigm, and "The depreciation of historical fact is deeply and probably functionally ingrained in the ideology of the scientific profession, the same profession that places the highest of all values upon factual details of other sorts."[18]

What does all this add up to? Kuhn himself calls attention to the fact that, except for the quotation from Francis Bacon, "the term 'truth'" is not used by him. Evolution is a process *"from* primitive beginnings," and that process can be described. "But nothing that has been or will be said makes it a process of evolution *toward* anything." Is there a need to assume that "some goal" has been "set by nature in advance"? On the contrary, "If we can learn to substitute evolution-from-what-we-do-know for evolution-toward-what-we-wish-to-know, a number of vexing problems may vanish in the process."[19] For

---

[17.] *Ibid.*, 125.
[18.] *Ibid.*, 137, 147.
[19.] *Ibid.*, 169 f.

many, Darwin's most significant contribution was the abolition of God and purpose, of teleological evolution.

Is it really necessary to know goals and purposes, if such exist? And "what must nature, including man, be like in order that science be possible at all?" This is a basic question, but Kuhn sees no need to answer it. "What must the world be like in order that man may know it?" Kuhn raises this question. As Van Til repeatedly answered, the only possible response leads straight to the ontological Trinity and the eternal decree. Kuhn is unwilling to answer the question. He is aware that presuppositions govern all thinking, and that scientific thinking rests on an eternal decree which gives law, structure, purpose, and meaning to all things. The basic paradigm is the eternal decree. But Kuhn suddenly becomes pragmatic in his conclusion, although in reality he always was:

> Any conception of nature compatible with the growth of science by proof is compatible with the evolutionary view of science developed here. Since this view is also compatible with close observation of scientific life, there are strong arguments for employing it in attempts to solve the host of problems that still remain.[20]

Modern science is thus schizophrenic. It operates on the basis of two mutually exclusive paradigms. *First*, it assumes the eternal decree, whereby, instead of brute, meaningless factuality, God's law establishes and undergirds all reality. *Second*, it assumes the autonomy of man as the sole source of law and meaning in a meaningless world.

In terms of its autonomy, modern science refuses to ascribe any goal or purpose to the universe. But, again in terms of its autonomy, it can visualize a scientifically guided and created goal. Thus Dandridge Cole believes that the goal is to be *macro-life, "a new form of gigantic size which has for its cells individual human beings, plants, animals and machines.* This is the kind of society or *being* which is likely to inhabit the moon and planetary colonies of the future."[21] In his *Politics*, Aristotle

---

20. *Ibid.*, 172.

defined man as a creature of the state, as a political animal. For these newer theorists, man is to be less a creature, merely a *cell*, of the scientific socialist state.

In other words, the choice is between God's absolute decree and man's absolute decree. By giving us an open choice about the question of purpose in the world, the scientists have given us a closed choice about themselves as absolute lords in terms of their purpose. Kuhn is right: paradigms, patterns, are inescapable. Man can only live in terms of paradigms. When Moses was admonished to "make all things according to the pattern shewed to thee in the mount" (Heb. 8:5), this pattern was simply a reflection of the total pattern and decree in terms of which all things were decreed and made by God (Acts 15:18).

This divine pattern or paradigm is denied by the modern evolutionary scientist. As a consequence, according to the Oakland, California, *Tribune* science writer, "The relentless juggernaut of science is swiftly shattering the world we know and generating a blizzard of ethical, moral, and legal problems which mankind is already being called upon to solve." However, it is not mankind but the scientists who feel called to offer a solution. A panel of the forty-eighth annual meeting of the American College of Physicians felt there was no divine paradigm or law, "no comfortable absolutes on which to rely in our moral dilemma, but rather that responsible choices have to be made by each of us as individuals as to an appropriate ethic or way of conduct in the ever shifting confrontation with the realities of our tension filled lives." So spoke Dr. Chauncey Leake of the University of California Medical Center. God's absolutes are ruled out, but man's absolutes are ruled in: "responsible choices have to be made" in terms of our independence and ultimacy, and, basically, these choices are to be determined by the scientific experts. Thus, Joshua Lederberg, professor of genetics at the Stanford University School of Medicine, feels that God's laws, as they relate to

---

21. Henry Still, *Will the Human Race Survive?* (New York: Hawthorne Books, 1966), 246.

abortion, are "savage." He denies to God any right to an absolute, even as he, Dr. Lederberg, pronounces one: "We cannot insist on absolute rights to life of a piece of tissue just because it bears a resemblance to humanity."[22] Take your choice, on abortion and all things else: the paradigm, pattern, law, or absolute of God, or that of Dr. Joshua Lederberg and his kind. You will live or die in terms of your decision.

An Associated Press report states that "Mankind stands on the threshold of 'playing God' because of the scientific breakthrough of the genetic code, a Michigan State University biophysicist believes." Dr. Leroy Augerstein predicted that this would occur "within 15 years."[23] We are very openly being given our choice of gods, the God of Scripture, or the new gods of science. And the scientists point to their own "power" with singular boastfulness; they have no doubts about themselves, however radical their doubts about Jesus Christ may be!

The late medieval period portrayed the priests as bloated parasites; it was a cruel caricature in part, but it was effective, because it had a strong element of truth. Later, monarchs came in for similar abuse; again; it was often unfair, but the aspect of arbitrariness did lend itself to caricature and attack. Sinclair Lewis, in *Elmer Gantry*, was also grossly unfair, and yet very successful, in that he put his finger on the egoism and lawlessness of evangelists. In recent years, the figure of the mad scientist has become commonplace, in comic strips, novels, and films. Again, the caricature is unfair and at the same time telling, in that it pinpoints the total lawlessness of scientists who have absolutized themselves and have seriously planned the remaking of humanity in terms of their imaginations. Their "dream of reason" is real, and it is madness. Moreover, it is logical. If men will not accept creationism, they cannot have the sovereignty of God. The revolutionary paradigm which

---

22. Jim Hazelwood, "The Shattering Impact of Science," Oakland, California, *Tribune*, 13 April 1967, 1.
23. "Man Ready to 'Play God,' Scientist Says," Los Angeles *Times*, 1 April 1967, 12.

will then govern men will be the "dream of reason," the paradigms of the autonomy and ultimacy of scientific man. The choice is between God's paradigm and man's paradigm, and men must reap the consequences of their choice. The widespread acceptance of Kuhn's paradigm clearly means that scientists have recognized their religious foundation, and they have self-consciously elected themselves as gods.

Chapter Twelve

The Revolution
of Rising Expectations

No more deadly mythology has ever plagued mankind than the mythology of science.

According to the Bible, with God all things are possible, but God does not choose to do all things for men. Men must face problems, moral choices, responsibilities, griefs, and disasters, and men must grow in terms of these things. The Bible makes abundantly clear God's miraculous power, but it makes equally clear the fact that man's first problem is his apostasy, his moral rebellion against God. Man needs salvation by God, growth in grace, and maturity as a pre-condition to prosperity under God. This world at its best involves work, and work under God's grace is blessed rather than cursed.

But according to the mythology of science, science can and will do all things. Not only are all things possible with science, but they are also planned for delivery. Sickness, disease, and death shall be abolished. Poverty, crime, and war shall be eliminated. Not only man, but also his world and weather shall be controlled. Life will be created, new organs, arms, and legs grown. The universe will be explored and populated, and, when the sun dies, a new sun shall be created and set in the heavens by our new gods, the scientists.

People believe this, some more, some less, but they do believe. They are fearful of these powerful new gods, and the fictional image of the mad scientist reflects a popular feeling. A god with total power and total purpose is rather a terrifying figure to many individuals.

But, however fearful they are of this new maker, people are entranced by his new creation, this brave new world promised by science. A politician of the new order spoke of this faith and its results as "the revolution of rising expectations." The phrase is an apt one. There is, all over the world, a revolution of rising expectations. When a workless, deathless world of peace and plenty is held to be within reach, the peoples will be satisfied with nothing less, and they will turn on, rend, and trample under foot those who give them less. Revolutionary discontent has become the order of the day. When men are taught to expect the life of the gods, they will not settle for the lot of man. When men believe that all things are attainable, they will accept nothing less. The result is a world-wide revolutionary dissatisfaction and discontent. Foreign aid can feed the unhappy masses, and provide them at times with more than they have known before, but man is now beyond happiness, because the revolution of rising expectations has made man insatiable. This new revolution therefore ensures a greater revolution; it ensures the collapse of all property and all law as it teaches men to despise the riches of the present for the promises of the future.

A brilliant scientist, who spent all his working years in charge of highly classified research, found himself troubled by the total experimentation of contemporary science, but he totally rejected the alternative of Christian faith. He believed in nothing but his science, and he feared it. Not too long before his untimely and almost suicidal death, he said bitterly, "If the people knew the kinds of things we are doing and planning with their tax money, they would take all scientists, line them up against a wall, and shoot them." He was wrong: the people would only ask for bigger grants to most projects. Any price would be worthwhile to gain the envisioned paradise of this new mythology. There would be momentary shock at some objectives, but the outcry would only be by way of atonement for basic consent. Let paradise come!

But the revolution of rising expectations can only culminate in the horror of disillusion, anarchy, and disaster. Then the self-righteous and consenting masses will cry for vengeance, forgetting that they too will be the objects of that vengeance.

"Except the LORD build the house, they labour in vain that build it" (Psalm 127:1). Since the rebuilding must be done, now is the time to begin Christian reconstruction.

Appendix One

The Myth of Nature

One of the major myths of the modern world is the idea that there is some such thing as "Nature," which the Second Edition of Merriam-Webster's Unabridged Dictionary defines as "a creative, controlling agent, force, or principle, or set of such forces or principles, operating or operative in a thing and determining wholly or chiefly its constitution, development, well-being, or the like," or "That which is produced by natural forces; the universe; as, laws governing *nature*; nothing happens without cause in *nature*; more narrowly, the totality of physical reality, exclusive of minds and the mental."

It is one thing to say that the universe or creation exists; it is another to assert that this universe is the source of its own laws and phenomena, or that it is a self-enclosed system of causality.

The Bible has no such term as "Nature." It does not recognize Nature as the source and cause of natural phenomena; rather, it sees God directly and absolutely operative in all natural phenomena. There is no law inherent in "nature," but there is a law over "nature." "Nature" is a collective name for an uncollectivized reality, and by uncollectivized it is meant that "nature" has no unity in and of itself that makes it a unified order. To assert that such a unity exists in and as "Nature" is to assert a hierarchical principle concerning the universe and its spheres.

If "nature" is a unity in status or in process, then it represents a system of higher and lower authorities, powers, and laws. It is subject to understanding in terms of its past, present, or continuing development as a scale of being in which there is both higher and lower being. The laws of that realm of being are to be derived from within the scale of being. If the primitive and lower is held to be more vital, then it is the true source of power and determination. If the rational and higher is held to be more important, then it becomes the necessary source of power and determination. In either case, causality and creative power are inherently located within the universe, and it becomes necessary to posit "Nature" as the ground of being, source of ultimacy, and "the system of all phenomena in space and time." If God is the Creator, then the system is not "Nature," but God's eternal decree.

To rule out the traditional concept of "Nature" means also to alter the traditional concept of the natural and the supernatural. In terms of the myth, the natural represents the normal life of a self-contained world system, whereas the supernatural is the intrusion of God's activity into that system. But if natural and supernatural events are both equally the activity of the triune God, and both equally His direct activity, then the distinction must be made on other grounds. The Bible does not hesitate to ascribe to God the storms, lightning, thunder, drought, plague, and other natural happenings in the same way that it ascribes the Virgin Birth and other miracles to Him. The Bible makes a vast distinction between the birth of men generally and the birth of Jesus Christ, but the difference is not to be found in locating God in the miracle and ascribing natural births to "nature." Rather, God is equally present in both; both are His direct decree, power, and action. The difference is not in the degree of God's presence or activity, but in the nature of the acts. The natural births represent God's pattern for mankind in its generation, whereas the Virgin Birth represents God's pattern for mankind in its regeneration. The Virgin Birth is unique, but it is still God's pattern or plan in terms of His eternal decree: mankind is miraculously given a new creation in Jesus Christ, and all who are reborn in Him are "born, not of blood, nor of the will of the flesh, nor of the will of man, but of God" (John 1:13).

The introduction of the concept of "Nature" and natural law, derived from Hellenic philosophy, led to a departure from Biblical faith. Natural law spoke of a self-contained system of its own inherent law. One of its products was Deism, which reduced God to the mechanic who merely created "Nature," and now "Nature" functioned independently of God. The next step was to accept the ultimacy of "Nature" and to drop God entirely.

The road to theistic recovery is only possible by a systematic attack on the illegitimate concept of "Nature," which imposes at the very least a screen of being between God and man, and, in its developed form, supplants God with a self-contained universe. "Nature" is a bastard concept and must be dropped.

Appendix Two

Review of Jan Lever's
Creation and Evolution

Jan Lever, *Creation and Evolution*[1], translated by Peter G. Berkhout (Grand Rapids International Publications, 1958), 244 pages.

This study, by a professor of zoology at the Free University at Amsterdam, is a detailed and mildly technical attempt to make the concept of evolution acceptable to creationists and to orthodox Christianity. As such, the arguments are of interest; and, even more interesting are the basic presuppositions of the author, which reveal a radical departure from Reformed philosophy.

Lever begins by ruling out, without offering any exegetical grounds, the creationist interpretation of Genesis 1 as "fundamentalistic," a name he insistently bestows on all who accept that interpretation. "Only, after this repudiation of fundamentalism, can we really approach the problem of the relationship between creation and evolution" (24). Since an approach to the problem is possible only after this repudiation,

[1.] First published in *Westminster Theological Journal*, vol. XXI, no. 2 (May 1959).

it follows that no serious attempt is made to understand the creationist interpretation, either exegetically, theologically, or scientifically. It is ruled out, as we shall see, as inherently impossible on *a priori* grounds, in terms of a particular philosophy.

For Lever, three possible interpretations exist. The first is "that all types of plants and animals in the progress of time have been created and that they possess only to a small degree the possibility of evolutionary development." The second is that only at certain points "in time were essentially new structures created: matter at the beginning, life after some time, the animal psyche later and the human spiritual structures only a relatively short time ago," with "further unfolding" following "a developmental process." The third possibility is that "all aspects of reality were created" in some beginning and subsequently evolved and came to realization (25).

A discussion of the question of spontaneous generation follows, with evidence collected to demonstrate that, throughout the centuries, especially in the medieval era, this concept was not considered as hostile to Christian faith. "People were free and for the most part without philosophical prejudice regarding this problem," comments Lever, evidently unaware of the extent to which Greek philosophical influences made Christian thinkers receptive to the idea of inherent potentiality in creation, whether in the form of spontaneous generation or monster births (36). In terms of their presuppositions, the fixity of species also was an alien concept. Lever clearly points out, however, that the scientific validity for the concept of spontaneous generation fell apart precisely when, with evolutionary thought, it became most necessary. The modern need for the idea has revived its consideration. Lever states that "the absence of data had the result that one's worldview could exercise influence upon scientific hypotheses with maximal resoluteness" (42). This sentence, and others like it, make questionable Lever's claim to represent Dooyeweerd's philosophy, for he regards the influence of pre-scientific thought as commensurate with the absence of scientific data, not as a pervasive and omnipresent fact of all thinking. He sees three possible hypotheses concerning the origin of life. "Since we have to deal with the question concerning the origin of lifeless material (A) and of life (B) and their reciprocal relation there are logically three possibilities: they are irrevocable (A + B); A is derived from B; or B is derived from A" (43). It should be noted that all three of these ostensibly logical possibilities presuppose a closed universe whose potentiality is inherent—again, hardly an idea to be ascribed to Dooyeweerd. On the basis of some highly nebulous reasoning from experiments of minimal import, Lever states, "it may be considered possible that various types of organic matter could originate upon the earth at the time when no life was present" (48). However, he does add that "it is very problematical whether (and if it is thus, how) large molecules such as proteins could form" (*ibid.*). But assuming that this did take place, the interpretations of the subsequent evolution are described as "practically entirely hypothetical" and as "only a scientific game invented by those who have accepted this worldview as their faith" (51). While pleading for evolution, Lever also gives some of the most telling evidence against it and candidly evaluates the weaknesses of the theory. Further discussing the origin of life, he again sees modern science presenting us with three speculations: (1) life "is as old as matter; (2) initially all matter was alive; (3) life came from lifeless matter." Which view is "purely scientific"? (52).

Before answering this question, Lever feels it necessary to rule out the idea of creation out of nothing as "an addition, a concoction," alien to Scripture (55). He sees "fundamentalism" or creationism as constantly leading to contradictions, but he forgets that evolution is built on contradictions. The Christian answer as developed by Lever is that "the essence of the entity of life in the organisms consists in its specific structure which was created 'in the beginning.' It is being realized constantly under God's guidance, along a line of (for us possibly improbable, but rightly) natural processes, since this entity of life was present in creation as possibility (we could also say, as necessity)" (57). Lever finds strict creationism to be as objectionable as the equivalently strict evolutionism. He seems to assume that God either added life to an already existing and eternal universe, or else guided what was present as possibility or necessity. What he wants, as the title of his last chapter indicates, is creation and evolution. But what part does creation play in this union? Creation, for Lever, is not historical, temporal, or scientifically discoverable. He rebels against any concept of creation which "drags the creation down into time." "The divine operation...does not permit itself to be scientifically discovered, indicated, dated and located within reality.... The creation is not periodically introduced into temporal reality, but it has produced, precisely through the power of God, this reality as a totality bounded by time. Creation precedes time" (208). Since a rejection of any "dualism" goes hand in hand with this concept, it becomes questionable whether God has any reality apart from the cosmos, and it is understandable why creation cannot be dated: it is bound up in the whole of reality as an aspect thereof, and not as an event resulting from a creative act by a sovereign and self-contained God. Hence, it is not surprising that Lever, abandoning an earlier reserve, eventually states that the purely scientific view is "that we as Christians should not consider it impossible that life originated by way of lifeless matter" (219). For him, Genesis has no meaning *as meaning*. A prominent poet has remarked that a poem should not *mean*; it simply *is*. In other words, it has a significance apart from meaning. Semantics, an extensive modern movement in the study of literature and religion (as well as in psychoanalysis), insistently denies meaning to meaning (expect in a scientific or critical context); meaning is an evasion of underlying truth, or a mythical expression of reality, or an independent expression not to be related to other areas. Always, another form of content rather than strict meaning is the valid one. This movement, often plausible, offers an easy escape from strict exegesis which too readily tempts even the best scholars.

In his study of "The Origin of the Type of Organism," Lever cites the self-consciously philosophic nature of evolutionary science. Yet, having noted this, he insists that "the data gathered by science naturally must be accepted. If we do not do that then we do violence to the truth and no science is possible" (93). He shows no willingness to separate philosophy and fact, or to weigh and admit the tentative or doubtful nature of most of the "facts," or to address the very great measure of actual slanting or falsifying of evidence by scientists, as in Haeckel, whom he cites extensively, and in the outright fraud of the Piltdown man.[2] Lever does make note of Dubois' dubious use of the so-called Java man, *Pithecanthropus erectus* (145). But, he never seems ready either to separate data and theory, or to recognize their identity. At this point, however, he does assert, inconsistently though, his conviction that "Although we do not know how this phyla-genesis has taken place, we are sure that it was not dominated by a purely closed immanent system, but it was purposefully directed and controlled by God" (99). In stating this certainty, Lever does not claim to give a scientific fact, but a faith which "leaves the way open for various scientific hypotheses" (*ibid.*).

In analyzing "The Concept of Species and the Problem of Origin" (chapter four), Lever reveals one of the main thrusts of his argument, an attempt to rule out the strict creationist point of view as Scholastic and Thomistic dualism. The doctrine of the fixity of species is for him neither Greek nor Christian, but strangely a product of the union of the two worldviews. How he squares this view of Thomism and Scholasticism with other evidence he cites as proof of medieval congeniality to spontaneous generation and the variableness of species, Lever does not say. He sees Hugo de Vries' "discovery of mutations" as the rescue of evolutionism, but he fails to state in what way mutations affect the fixity of species. De Vries' work with *Oenothera Lamarckiana*, the evening primrose, revealed mutations which produced no new species but only varieties

---

[2.] See J. S. Weiner, *The Piltdown Forgery* (Oxford: Oxford University Press, 1955), 150. This "falsification" is noted by Lever.

which bred out recessive characteristics. Most mutations prove harmful to the organism. Much of the trouble in the species problem is the difficulty of definition, combined with an abiding recognition of necessity for that classification, despite recurring attempts to eliminate it. Laboratory experiments have produced new species (that is, species breeding true to type and infertile with both parents), but these are still not proof of evolution, in that, tomatoes, for example, still remain tomatoes. Kinds and species are not to be strictly identified, although a close relationship does exist. But any kinds-species relationship or creationist fixity is objectionable to Lever, who wants the Christian biologist to "be liberated from every form of cold and nihilistic determinism" (140).

Lever gives much attention to the origin of man (chapter five). His account is a cautious one, dubious of the fanciful simianized reconstructions. He understands the development, as far as the evidence permits us to see, to be one of essentially cultural rather than biotic evolution. As far as we know, man has always been man. But Lever will not permit his reader to use this evidence to bolster his faith in Genesis, because "we may never demand from Scripture exact physical, astronomical, biological and thus also not exact historical knowledge" without being "fundamentalistic" (170f.). At the same time, and very inconsistently, Lever objects to any attempt to deny "factually real significance" to Genesis, and pronounces it "senseless to confront the scientific results with the Bible" (170). And yet this is precisely Lever's own position. He denies to Genesis any "scientific-historical historicity" and states, "consequently the genealogies similarly have not the same historical correctness, as, e.g., the family tree of the Royal House of the Netherlands, as it is found in the history books" (177). Thus Scripture gives us neither science nor history. For Lever, Scripture deals with reality in terms of categories and principles: "it is our opinion that Genesis has been written to reveal realities for us that are of eternal, fundamental religious significance and which cannot be discovered through science. These revealed realities we should accept gratefully and we should lay them as normative at the basis also of our scientific thinking. These revealed realities have no *concrete* contact with our investigation. They cannot be investigated and they cannot be imprisoned in our scientific-human concepts" (21). For this Lever feels "we should be grateful"! (22). We shall see later how Lever, who deems dualism a cardinal sin, has created two worlds (similar to Plato's), one of ideas and the other of matter, and can find neither conflict nor link between them. Thus, in spite of his own evidence to the contrary, evolution must be true for Lever because to believe in creation, i.e., in Scripture the historically of, would be a violation of his Biblical, religious, and philosophical principles. For him God cannot act in this manner. For him, Genesis is "a religious revelation" from which "we may not read...a scientific statement about the 'how' of the origin of man, but only a revelation *that* man owes his existence to creation and that in every respect he is linked with that which has been created" (196). Since "created" and "creation" are words of such vague meaning to Lever, we might add that this revelation adds up to little or nothing. The identification of man as merely "a peculiar kind of animal," the justification of war as the survival of the fittest, and the comparison of human society to animal society and similar evolutionary interpretations, Lever rejects as "excess, undoubtedly not wished by the best representatives of evolutionism," and as "*doctrine*" and "*dogma*" (191). Why the whole theory cannot be dismissed as well, in view of the lack of evidence, he does not say. [It is classified as dogma by a scientist, Anthony Standen, in a very properly titled study, *Science is a Sacred Cow* (Dutton, 1958), 100ff].

It would be too lengthy a process to specifically criticize Lever in terms of the many individual bits of data. One could point out, for example, that he shows no critical awareness of de Vries' methodology in redefining species by viewing them, in de Vries' own words, "in the light of the doctrine of descent"; in other words, accept an unproven hypothesis as true, and use it as an assumption with which to prove a second hypothesis. The second is then used to prove the truth of the first hypothesis! The significance of Mendel is hardly appreciated. But central to much of Lever's thinking, and something which cannot be bypassed, is his assumption of the validity of the time-scheme of modern science, which, despite its wide variety of dating (what's a few billion years between scientists?), is accepted as true. But is the evolutionary time-scheme actually necessary? Lever does not discuss the dating methods. They are various: erosion-deposition (for the earth), the uranium time clock, the meteorite method, the fluoride dating of organic remains, and radioactive-carbon dating. All these depend on a variety of assumptions which are in themselves questionable, so that none can be regarded as even remotely safe. Too many factors contribute to their instability. Some writers can and do use the same methods, for example the uranium time clock, to assert both relatively recent and far-distant dates of the earth. The uranium time clock depends on a number of assumptions which are themselves unprovable and without evidence. For example, the original nature of the rock must be assumed as known; in terms of this assumption alone, one can, depending on his views of that original nature, derive a date varying from hundreds of millions of years to no more than twenty or thirty thousand years, employing, in either instance, equally accurate measurements. The plain fact is that, while some data suggest a recent date and some do not, the evidence is as yet inconclusive. But evolutionism cannot permit such uncertainty. The billions of years in the evolutionary time scheme are an equivalent and substitute for God; diluted by time and chance, scientifically incredible miracles are given enough margin of opportunity to work the impossible. Thus, as each successive dating method proves untenable, others are created; meanwhile, the time scheme remains as the central fact. The situation is similar to the medieval proofs of God; the proofs failed, but God remained. The dating methods also fail, but the time scheme must go on; as the substitute and equivalent for God it is a philosophical necessity. It is a faith construct.

Lever's book has been compared to Ramm's *The Christian View of Science and Scripture,* and a note here is important. Apart from calling creationists "fundamentalists" and using this designation as a term of insult, Lever does not share Ramm's insistent abuse of creationists. Perhaps most of us have at some time or other wished that Scripture said more, less, or otherwise than it does on some particular point, but to allow such a wish to govern our interpretation is dangerous, to say the least. With both Ramm and Lever, the concern is not to interpret the Word of God in Genesis strictly and accurately, letting the chips fall where they may, but to interpret it in such a manner as to satisfy both their desire for Christian orthodoxy *and* scientific orthodoxy. The result is greater interest in *latitude* than in *exegesis.* Thus, only a harmonizing interpretation is tolerable for Ramm, not the Word of God in itself, and Ramm can write, "for those supernatural events with reference to astronomical matters there are one or more credible, reasonable interpretations which should cause no embarrassment to any man with a scientific mentality but also with Christian convictions" [168; cf. 342. "This theory would relieve us of the problem of time reduction." For a similar approach, see N. H. Ridderbos, *Is There a Conflict Between Genesis and Natural Science?* (Eerdmans, 1957), 46: "The fact that there arise objections of a scientific nature to every more literal conception may and should occasion the question, Is it perhaps possible to offer some other acceptable exegesis?"]. But, if we remove every interpretation objectionable to science, philosophy, or human consciousness in general, what gospel have we left? Is it not precisely the nature of the gospel that it is an offense to autonomous reason at every point, because its every presupposition is alien to the natural man? This indifference to strict and careful exegesis is shared by Lever; he is not here concerned with the actual meaning of the biblical text but with his own theory of it, which he feels is more capable of being fundamentally Christian (5), so indicating that his own conception of fundamental Christianity is here radically at odds with Scripture. Lever, by reinter-preting Scripture to eliminate historic creationism, also eliminates any true fall; his conception of primitive religion is evolutionary; no fall is presupposed. And yet he hopes to retain the fall as a Christian doctrine (217f.) and speaks of man's original (but not historical) powers over nature. He absorbs "the divine guidance by the evolving unfolding of the flora and fauna, of human life and culture, or of the re-creation in Jesus Christ" all equally into a concept of miracles which "are not amenable to sense-perception and they cannot be the object of experimentation or proof" (231). Thus, ultimately, evolution is absorbed into revelation and made a dogma of faith. The scientific compulsion to accept evolution is therefore ultimately a dogma that lacks even a revealed order of appearance or a scriptural basis, but it must be accepted nevertheless. Certainly no one dare accuse Lever of any lack of faith.

Basic to Lever's thinking is an unbiblical dualism. There is a separation of faith and fact, as though they existed in two separate worlds. Reason and revelation are likewise separated, as are God and creation (when they are not merged). There is usually for Lever no comprehensible relationship or provable contact between the two realms. For the most part, the world of data gives only evolutionary proof (although, here again, inconsistently, he finally absorbs evolution into the realm of revelation and miracle); the world of data is capable only of anti-theistic factuality. But theism must rest on a non-historical and non-scientific revelation, Scripture, which lacks the historical validity of a Dutch history book. (Lever thus is only one degree removed from neo-orthodox thinking, which understands the Virgin Birth and resurrection as revelation and religiously necessary but historically untrue.) Thus, for Lever facts are not God-created facts; they cannot be God-interpreted, because revelation must not be forced into an historical mold. He must, then, hold one thing to be scientifically true of data, another to be religiously true. Thomas Aquinas, while holding that revelation alone could penetrate the spiritual world, judged reason capable of validly interpreting the physical universe, thus assuming the self-sufficiency of reason in its own domain. How has Lever escaped this? Has he not rather "out-Thomased" Aquinas? Lever holds the fixity of species to be a scholastic and Greek idea on the ground that to be unchanging means to be an idea, a form. Shall we then conclude that the concept of an unchanging and self-contained God is only an idea? Certainly Lever gives no evidence of appreciating the significance of the doctrine of the self-contained and ontological Trinity. His sharp distinction between theology and philosophy, between faith and science, has marked kinship to the modern Kantian and neo-orthodox approach. Apologetically, the presuppositions of Scripture are used; this is the realm of faith. Exegetically and scientifically, the presuppositions of natural man are used; this is the realm of reason and science. This is, unhappily, too much in evidence among some of the men of Amsterdam. It appears in Berkouwer and is responsible for his favorable approach to Barth. It appears in N. H. Ridderbos, who can affirm the orthodox doctrines and hold critical views of Genesis. And Dooyeweerd's great and valuable work contains a concept of time which removes "the initial words of the book of Genesis" from historical time, as Gordon H. Clark has pointed out ["Cosmic Time: a Critique of the Concept in Herman Dooyeweerd" in *Gordon Review*, vol. II, no. 3 (September 1956), 94-95].

According to Lever, then, Christianity must work with one set of axioms, and science with another: "The origin of organisms occurred intentionally and ran its course according to a plan, even though from a scientific point of view we can record only chance-processes" (56). How the intentional course can exist in the natural realm without making it necessary for science to operate in recognition of it, Lever does not explain. Here, as elsewhere, he is philosophically confused. While Lever appeals at times to Kuyper and Dooyeweerd, he is by no means in their tradition. His book, though hardly likely to affect Biblical interpretation, is likely to do much

harm in being used to bring discredit on Kuyper and
Dooyeweerd, whose works, while certainly representing no
final system and having points in need of correction, do
certainly indicate the true direction for Reformed thinking.

There is no recognition on Lever's part that two worldviews
are in collision in the doctrines of creation and evolution. He
sees the controversy as one resulting from the conflict of
ignorance with science. Arnold Lunn has called attention to
the fact that evolution prospered and met with welcome in
Darwin's day because it satisfied the theophobia, the fear and
dislike of God, of that day: pure chance was regarded as
preferable to God [*Is Evolution Proved?* A debate between
Douglas Dewar and H. S. Shelton, intro. by Arnold Lunn
(Hollis and Carter, 1947), 4]. Robert E. D. Clark has also noted
this in *Darwin: Before and After* (Paternoster Press, 1950, 90 ff.)
and has called attention to the important fact that evolution
created a revolution within science, a revolt against exact
science in favor of theory and philosophy (*ibid.*, 76ff). More
than that, it must be added that Darwin's theory, contrary to
popular mythology, did not result in a conflict between
theology and science. With exceptions, churchmen by and
large found Darwin's theory a welcome relief, and the church,
dead to its core, took more readily to Darwin than did science,
where some real resistance occurred. Only subsequently,
especially towards the end of the century, did real theological
opposition emerge, however fragmentarily, and only in our
generation is it beginning to develop theologically and
philosophically. Why the success of evolutionary theory? This
writer, who was reared in evolutionary thinking and once
regarded it as one of life's certainties, found his confidence in
it destroyed in his university days, not only because it lacked
any evidence, but also because he recognized that evolutionary
thinking is mythological thinking, that the theory is a cultural
myth. Both Darwin and Wallace found their theory, not in
observations of nature, but in Malthus' *Essay on Population*,
and in the economic theory of *laissez-faire* survival of the
fittest; both acknowledged the debt. The political-economic

world of their day is faithfully mirrored by Darwin and Wallace, and their theory had the ring of infallible and irresistible truth to that generation. The appeal of a world of chance as against responsibility to a sovereign God continues, and autonomous reason claims the theory to be as necessary as truth. Darwinism, however, is now as "out-of-date" to "thinking man" as the clothing, economics, and imperialism of that day; newer styles command the attention and feed the myth. In this age of revolution and of contempt for the principle of legitimate authority, historic law, constitutionalism, and continuity, evolutionary theory has discarded the necessity for development and the attempt to discover intermediate forms. In its place, discontinuities are seen as evidence of evolution, as natural jumps in development. Nothing changes the myth, nor discourages it; its outward manifestation varies in conformity to the general cultural pattern, but at its heart is the unchanging affirmation of pure chance and the autonomy of man at any price.

In this conflict there can be no compromise; in terms of this conflict, Lever's work is a masterpiece of irrelevancy, a confused, albeit well-intentioned work whose real danger may be that it brings discredit upon the Reformed philosophy it erroneously claims to represent. For Lever is not Reformed. No Reformed thinker can reduce reality to a dead sea of factuality. No Reformed thinker can insist that God must be excluded from our scientific thinking on the ground that, otherwise, we believe in "'intervention by metaphysical factors'" and "reduce God to an instrument of our thinking, a *deus ex machina* that we call to our aid to help us solve the critical points in our thinking" (208). For truly Reformed thinkers, God, as the creator of all things, is their only valid interpreter, and His infallible Word gives the truth concerning all factuality. Apart from Scripture and the ontological Trinity, no fact can be truly known. To attempt to study facts in terms of "chance-processes" is to know nothing, and a scientific point of view which seeks to record only chance-processes can, if strictly honest in adhering to its presuppositions, record nothing. One cannot be Reformed while holding to a worldview which is inoperative.

For Lever, revelation and the reality of nature "constitute one transaction" (177). But if so, then revelation is nothing in itself, and ultimately God is nothing in Himself. And this is precisely what the modern Kantian distinction between theology and philosophy, between revelation and science, tends to accomplish. It veers between an identification and a total separation, because it either loses itself in the dead sea of factuality or in the undifferentiated void of one meaningless universal or reality. Lever asks us to sell our birthright, but does not offer even a mess of pottage in return!

Appendix Three

Review of Mixter's
Evolution and Christian Thought Today

Russell L. Mixter, editor, *Evolution and Christian Thought Today*[1]. Grand Rapids: Wm. B. Eerdmans Publishing Co. 1959. 224 pages + 16 plates.

This symposium by thirteen authors, published for the November 1959 centennial of Darwin's *The Origin of Species*, is an appraisal of the theory of evolution by members of the American Scientific Affiliation (A.S.A.), whose purpose "is to study those topics germane to the conviction that the frameworks of scientific knowledge and a conservative Christian faith are compatible." Each of these essays was subjected to critical review by every other author and revised accordingly. As a summary of the present status of thinking in the various branches of science discussed, this volume is outstanding. While the articles, being of necessity elementary in their treatment, give no indication of the competence of the authors in their respective fields of research, they do give evidence of greater balance and perspective than is displayed

---

[1] Reprinted from *Westminster Theological Journal*, vol. XXIII, no. 1 (November 1960).

by some prominent specialists in these fields. Indeed, from the scientific perspective, the restraint and caution with which the data are studied is the most prominent and noteworthy characteristic of this symposium.

From the Biblical perspective, the situation is less commendable, nor is there the same respect for Biblical data as for scientific reports. Despite the earnestly professed adherence to the Christian faith, a treatment of Scripture which is practically cavalier prevails. Indeed, the title is scarcely justified, in that the Christian aspect is lightly regarded by the scientists, and is, in the main, left to the theologian, Carl F. H. Henry. As an oft-repeated instance of this, notice George K. Schweitzer's statement: "Biblical language is not the precise language of modern-day science; it is popular, phenomenal, and oft-times poetical. Thus we are not to look for intricate detail, but for basic underlying principles" (47). Others likewise speak of Genesis 1 in similar terms, as witness Walter R. Hearn and Richard A. Hendry, who see it as "a brief but beautifully poetic narrative" which "gives little specific information about the ways in which God has worked in nature, possibly because such details are irrelevant to the major theme of his revelation of himself" (67f). For them, "the legitimate question of limitations imposed by the actual words of Scripture" is easily answered: "The authors of this chapter consider the expressions in Scripture regarding the creation of life to be sufficiently figurative to imply little or no limitation on possible mechanisms. Others may disagree with this conclusion" (69). But is "figurative" language an evasion of meaning, or is it not rather an instrument of clarification and a type of precision? This "poetic" and hence loose and general sense of Scripture is frequently referenced. In view of the fact that Jesus rested the doctrine of life after death on the tense of a verb (Mark 12:18-27) and Paul the covenant of faith on the singular form of seed (Gal. 3:16), it must be asserted that Scripture speaks precisely, even if it does not use the language of the laboratory, which is very far from being the only form of precision. If poetic language eliminates strict interpretation in favor of only "basic underlying principles," then what happens to the doctrine of the Virgin Birth? Genesis one is highly propositional in contrast to Matthew 1-2 and Luke 2. The unhappy fact is that Genesis 1 has, in almost every age, been approached with the theological, philosophical, and scientific presuppositions of that age and accordingly interpreted, rather than being permitted, with the whole of Scripture, to provide those presuppositions. It is to be feared that these men refuse to acknowledge any interpretation of Genesis 1-11 which might put them at radical odds with contemporary science.

The basic defect of these studies, however, is philosophical, and then scientific and theological. There is a radical absence of a consistent Christian philosophy of science. Henry, in his essay, written with a gentlemanly restraint of criticism for his scientific fellow-writers, nevertheless observes, "What Christian thinkers unfortunately have failed to do is to elaborate a schematic philosophy of science based on revealed theism, from which standpoint forceful questions can be levelled at the competitive secular philosophy of science" (220). The A.S.A. was very recently summoned to consider the elements of such a philosophy in a forthright and powerful statement of "The Need for an Evangelical Philosophy of Science" by Thomas H. Leith [*Journal of the American Scientific Affiliation* (December 1959): 3-13]. Let us briefly review some of Leith's comments. He cites Alexander Ross in 1646 as calling attention to the unhappy status of factuality: "'Whereas you say that astronomy serves to confirm the truth of Holy Scripture you are very preposterous; for you will have the truth of Scripture confirmed by astronomy, but you will not have the truth of astronomy confirmed by Scripture; sure one would think that astronomic truths had more need of Scriptural confirmation than the Scripture of them'" (*ibid.*, 7). What is this needed confirmation? Leith states it clearly:

> As a man sows his axioms so shall he reap his deductions. No one can validly *deduce* more than that with which he begins. If he does not start with God as sovereign he will

not end up with Him. Nor can a man *induce* the Biblical God from observations in nature. A God who *might* act in nature doesn't prove that He did. Also, God is not exhausted in His natural revelation and it is thus insufficient to give all truth about Him as Hume pointed out long ago (*ibid.*, 10).

Man's criteria, insists Leith, can only be derived from God Himself, and a Baconian science which claims to approach factuality without preconceptions is a "figment of the imagination." "Scripture must be seen as the unique revelation of the Archimedian point of truth which is God." "Hence the propositions of Scripture become axioms in a truly Christian Philosophy" (*ibid.*, 10-12). This view, so ably expounded and safeguarded by Leith, has been extensively developed by Cornelius Van Til and Herman Dooyeweerd, and is defended by others.

The approach of this symposium on *Evolution and Christian Thought Today* is radically different. According to Hearn and Hendry:

> Scientific investigations must always be mechanistic in their outlook, because it is only in this narrowed frame of reference that the scientific method can operate. It is probably true that many non-believers have welcomed mechanistic interpretations of this phenomena, and especially of the origin of life, feeling that such interpretations would make belief in God unnecessary. Such an attitude is indicative of a basic misunderstanding of the Christian idea of God and the way by which we come to know him. Belief in God is never forced upon us, no matter what our level of understanding of natural processes. God cannot be found by scientific knowledge any more than he can by scientific ignorance. The mechanistic view and the teleological, philosophical, or theological view of nature are complementary to each other and not antithetical (69).

J. Frank Cassel expresses his dissent from this statement, declaring, "A Christian's assumptions or presuppositions must be Christian," but fails to develop this thesis consistently (163). For it is not enough to hold a Christian faith: the concepts of factuality and hypothesis as maintained by contemporary scientific thought are consistently anti-Christian. If it be true that God is the Creator, and that "the heavens declare the glory of God; and the firmament showeth his handiwork," then all factuality makes an inevitable witness which man either accepts or evades (Ps. 19:1). According to Paul, "the invisible things of him since the creation are clearly seen," and unbelievers "hold down" the truth in unrighteousness (Rom. 1:20; 1:18; "hold down" or "holding down" is considered to be the meaning by Kenneth S. Wuest, and many other scholars). To begin with this presupposition involves holding to a radically different concept of fact and hypothesis from that of scientists who believe in a world of brute factuality, a world lacking design, causality, or purpose, and to be understood in terms of basically mechanistic or naturalistic processes. Such a concept prejudges the outcome far more than do Christian presuppositions, which require a humility before God-given factuality and an honesty with regard to the God-given interpretation of factuality.

But what is the approach of the symposium? Wilbur L. Bullock, writing in *The Gordon Review* [reprinted as "Evolution and/or Creation," in *Eternity* (July 1960): 10-12, 31], states, "We must always be willing to examine and alter our position in order to be as faithful as we know how to *both* God's words and God's works even though this may make us unpopular with our non-Christian colleagues or with our non-Christian friends" (31). Thus, "God's words and God's works" are put on an equality, Scripture and science as equal and either complementary or competing sources. But Scripture cannot be so equated without damage to faith; it does not ask to be a substitute for observation but to govern the presuppositions of observation. In actual practice, the writers of the symposium base their observations on radically anti-Christian premises and then try to harmonize the results with Christian doctrine, so that Scripture "comes in" a very lame second. Bullock himself gives evidence of this harmonization in his statement concerning Darwin's concepts of natural selection and survival of the fittest: "But such a proposition is just the naturalistic way of expressing the theological concept of the providence of God" (119)! The truth of the matter is that Darwin's concept is the naturalistic *substitute* for God's providence, and a *substitute* concept or *imitative* concept is as much at odds with the reality as Fuhrer Hitler was with Messiah Jesus. Donald S. Robertson and John Sinclair write:

> In evaluating the contribution of genetics to evolution and its significance to the Christian, we must remember that the scientist has assumed a mechanistic universe which he feels can be understood if properly observed and analyzed. His working hypothesis while engaged in scientific endeavor has no room for a God that can fortuitously interrupt his smoothly working machine. Since this is the working hypothesis of science, it was only a matter of time before theistic explanations of origins were abandoned in favor of mechanistic ones. Thus the theory of evolution came along as an inevitable consequence of the scientific procedure (89).

After this observation, we hopefully look for some recognition that, because evolution is "the inevitable consequence of the scientific procedure" on mechanistic and anti-theistic lines, there is need for the reinstitution of Christian presuppositions, and we expect that a radical re-evaluation on those premises will follow. Instead, we find God banished from science! According to Robertson and Sinclair,

> In conclusion, it is interesting to note that it is impossible to demonstrate God's creative activity from within the realm of scientific discovery, just as it is also impossible to demonstrate his sustaining activity. However, these relationships of God to his creation are not anti-scientific just because they cannot be demonstrated by science. They are concepts that are outside the realm in which science operates and thus science has little if anything to say about their validity. These are questions that must be answered by faith (91).

But God can never be "demonstrated" by any activity or system which begins by eliminating Him. And the Christian claim is not that God can be demonstrated by the facts, but that no facts can be explained or demonstrated apart from God, that what knowledge the covenant-breaker has he holds on borrowed premises, because, as Van Til has ably and repeatedly pointed out, on consistently non-Christian premises no knowledge is possible. The concluding sentence of Robertson and Sinclair is especially revealing: "These are questions that must be answered by faith." Some questions are answered, according to this symposium, by science, and others by faith. Hence their insistence, in order to give science free rein, on the "poetic" nature of Scripture: it would be upsetting to take creation and the flood in too strict a sense, and it must be insisted, whatever the textual reading, that a loose sense is the best scientific and religious sense.

There is thus a realm for science and a realm for faith. But how to join the two? Sinclair has tried doing just that in an essay on "New Genes" [*Journal of American Scientific Affiliation* (December 1955): 12-14]. To this, T. Hinton, Department of Zoology, University of California at Los Angeles, made answer:

> In my opinion, it is never fitting for a true scientist to deviate from the natural cause explanation. If some god can create new genes out of nothing at will, then there is no point in any of us seeking the basis of life. And as long as there is any doubt in Mr. Sinclair's mind then he certainly is in the wrong field. His reasoning is very similar to that of the communists who decided that since a supernatural force was indicated, genes could not exist— this is very dangerous reasoning (*ibid.*, 14).

In terms of Hinton's definition, none of the authors of the symposium is a "true scientist." They begin uniformly on mechanistic premises and seek a natural cause explanation. In this scheme of things, God is a total outsider, and He can only become another name for man's ignorance. Both progressive creationism (evolution with a more pious name) and theistic evolution fail to commend themselves to scientists because they are bastard products, representing a crossing of two hostile strains, which produces a sterile offspring. The authors have no desire for conflict between the two strains; it is hardly conducive professionally to advancement. But the results of their forced union are only productive of frailty or sterility.

Although we are told that the authors are all "committed to the evangelical Christian doctrine that the world and its living members are the result of the activity of God as declared in the Holy Scriptures," their outward and emotional adherence to evangelical Christianity does not erase the fact that they are intellectually and scientifically Thomistic in their thinking (6). Indeed, this volume is a better exposition of Thomistic principles than the Duquesne *Symposium on Evolution* (1959). According to Thomism, the reason of autonomous man is capable of impartially and objectively investigating the truths of creation, by means of philosophy, science, and other disciplines, and only in certain areas, where investigation is impossible, do revelation and faith enter in to supplement reason. The inevitable consequence of this approach, which made man's science independent and autonomous, was to render God only another name for ignorance or the unknown, and thus hardly anything deserving of faith. As a result, Occam's philosophical razor neatly removes God from the picture as rightly irrelevant and unnecessary. For this symposium, the methodology and underlying philosophy of factuality, hypothesis, and rationality are derived from contemporary science and presuppose a system in which God is by definition irrelevant and merely a name for ignorance. Hinton's objection is basically sound, for we cannot switch axioms and presuppositions in midstream. We cannot have one set of premises for our observations and another for our conclusions, as these authors insist on doing.

It will not do to point to the similarities between providence and Darwin's hypothesis. Much more indeed can be pointed out: the Darwinian and evolutionary concept of natural processes "out-miracles" God, in that built-in miracles and omnipotence are presupposed at every step in a blind and insentient process. The evolutionary concept of the universe requires a faith in comparison to which Biblical Christianity requires but little, but the evolutionary faith is ready to swallow camels and retain man's autonomy rather than face the offense of accountability and Godly creaturehood.

These men are evangelical churchmen and Thomistic scientists, an untenable and compartmentalized situation, basically schizoid in nature. They are aware that evolution is by no means proven and may indeed, by the nature of the case be unprovable, but for them its validity remains because the presuppositions of their science call for such an explanation. This leads to peculiar statements, as witness the following by James O. Buswell, III:

> One of the chief drawbacks to the anti-evolutionists, from Darwin's early critics to the present day (familiar as some of their leaders are with the data), is that their activities and literature have been almost completely wrapped up in arguments over petty fragments of the record, assuming that to attack evolution as a total philosophy one must show the data upon which the assumptions are based to be untrue (169).

Before analyzing this amazing statement, it should be noted that Buswell stands out for his willingness to admit that not all creationists must be considered ignorant and "obnoxiously anti-cultural, anti-educational, and anti-scientific," the "hyper-orthodox" of Ramm's account (cited by Buswell, 168ff.). That some opponents of evolution have been such is clearly true, but a fair reading of the past century's history will place the burden of offense with evolutionists. By and large, the symposium's writers find Ramm's *Christian View of Science and Scripture* very much to their taste.

But to return to Buswell's statement, which says, in effect, "Don't confuse the issue with facts." It seems we are in error in "assuming that to attack evolution as a total philosophy one must show the data upon which the assumptions are based to be untrue." (169) It should be noted that this statement, like every other, was subjected to the editorial scrutiny of every writer (5). What then is evolution? The writers want it both as a body of impartial observations of nature, open to universal examination, and as a philosophy which is a faith beyond facts and incapable of disproof. At every point, mixed premises predominate, and "scientific creationism" is the strange result. Moreover, it is frequently inferred that because changes have taken place in nature and these changes *can* be called evolution, we are therefore, if honest, compelled to accept some kind of evolution! By a marvelous process of redefinition, we are all made "evolutionists" on penalty of dishonesty; men can all be made believers in "God" by the same process of redefinition, but it is doubtful if either the cause of science or faith is promoted by such an approach. Even Bullock, who protests against the equation of speciation and evolution by "the average evolutionist" as "unfair," still writes in *The Gordon Review* and *Eternity*, "As the theory of evolution encompasses, in part, the small changes which all must accept, it follows that we must admit some evolution has taken place" (121; *Eternity*, 12).

We are repeatedly asked to make a leap of faith from inconclusive data to evolution. For example, Irving W. Knobloch, after a very careful and conscientious survey of what is called "The Role of Hybridization in Evolution" but is actually a survey of hybridization as such, declares, "If hybridization plays only a minor role in evolution, as some maintain, it is very strange indeed that there are so many vigorous, fertile hybrids in existence today, and more being found each year by those who earnestly search for them" (103). To "prove" hybrids is one thing, to "prove" evolution is another. Again, to demonstrate the reality of one is not to demonstrate the reality of the other unless by definition everything constitutes proof of the basic presupposition. Knobloch has only demonstrated, in terms of a particular approach, that hybrids exist. More than that he has not shown. In view of the complexity of the problem of defining species, the problem of hybrids is correspondingly difficult. The phenomenon is real, but what is it? Knobloch himself clearly states, "There have been almost as many definitions of a species as there are biologists" (94). Does the present state of knowledge permit the extensive theorizing so prevalent on every side of the issue? The authors are cautious in their surveys of the present state of research, far more so than most writers. But in stating conclusions, they tend to abandon that reserve.

V. Elving Anderson writes to the issue in stating that "evangelical Christians need a basic outlook which will permit them to view the growing body of scientific data and hypotheses without fear or hesitation, but with considerable interest and anticipation. This will be possible only as we continue to develop a comprehensive philosophy of science, a statement of the ways in which God is, and has been related to the universe" (134). He finds such a philosophy pointed to by Taylor Lewis in Lewis' statement, "'It is because the Scripture doctrine of the Word, or Logos, in nature, has so fallen out of our theology, that we dread so much the appearance of naturalism'" (135; the citation from Lewis is from J. P. Lange, *Genesis*, translated and with additions by Taylor Lewis and A. Gosman). Carl Henry echoes this emphasis in one clearly unhappy aspect of his essay on "Theology and Evolution" and looks for integration "through the recovery of the Logos as the key to creation, revelation, redemption, sanctification, and judgment—in other words, as the center of reference for science, philosophy, religion, ethics, and history" (221). But the *Logos* as a *principle* has been used, and its abstract nature has led to a destruction of Christian categories, as witness some patristic thinking. In Thomistic hands, following Aristotle, the *Logos* as *structure* brought back meaning to the universe, but it cut loose from God, and faith was given only the areas of mystery beyond the universe. The *Logos* tends to be understood as either an abstract universal emptying the world of meaning, or as a concrete universal, which, as the basic principle, incarnates meaning in the universe and empties eternity of meaning. Neo-orthodoxy, by its use of Christ-, or *Logos*-, centered philosophy, has tried to bridge the gap, but has only succeeded in exhausting God in His relational aspect, and thereby reabsorbing all into flux and relativity and confounding itself. The *Logos* in isolation from His ultimate context becomes an emptied context. The ontological Trinity is alone the safe-ground for philosophy and the only key to knowledge, as Van Til has elucidated.

We regret that *Evolution and Christian Thought Today* cannot be commended. Its writers are able men, and the purpose of the American Scientific Affiliation an attractive one. It would be a delight to have the opportunity to praise their work. But the unhappy fact is that the group is a better exponent of Thomism than of Biblical Christianity. Even the name reflects this. It is motivated, not by cowardice or by a lust for academic respectability, but by an earnest faith according to which these authors are scientists like every other scientist, carrying on research on the same premises, the only difference between them being religious rather than "scientific." This equation and sense of common ground is the essence of Thomism. But can a consistent Christian be a Thomist, and should he be a member of an implicitly Thomistic society? The name and the approach typify a philosophy which seeks to escape the offense of Biblical faith but succeeds only in escaping its victory.

Appendix Four

Duquesne University Symposium on Evolution

(Review article, reprinted from *Torch and Trumpet*, October 1960[1])

No better witness to the triumph of Charles Darwin's thesis in his *Origin of Species* could have been given than this symposium held at Duquesne University, April 4, 1959. Four devout scholars of the Church of Rome, a botanist, anthropologist, philosopher, and theologian, unite in interpreting evolution in terms of a congeniality on the part of Rome. Bernard J. Boelen, Duquesne professor of philosophy, assures us in the introduction that Darwin was a warm-hearted, good, just, and lovable man, and his theory a "challenge" to the church, established as it is by Darwin "on a factual basis." Boelen, like the others, is hostile to "the literal interpretation of the Book of Genesis in the sense of creationism." "Life has existed on earth for more than a billion years" and man must reckon with this reality in his religious thinking (3-8).

---

[1]. *Duquesne University Symposium on Evolution.* Intro. by B. J. Boelen. Articles by C. Bawden, Andrew J. Melden, Gottfried O. Lang, Cyril Vollert, S. J., (Pittsburgh, Oh.: Duquesne University, 1959), 119 pp. Imprimatur, Archbishop Edward J. Hunkeler.

Frederick C. Bawden, in discussing "Evolution and Viruses," believes that evolution, "open to objective tests...stands now even more firmly established" than one hundred years ago (11). His study of viruses, however, adds nothing to the question, since he believes viruses to be "relatively late products of evolution rather than primitive forms" (15). Gottfried O. Lang, the anthropologist, similarly adds nothing to the subject except a quick survey in which evolution is assumed, and then evidence searched and "facts" seen only in relation to an assumed theory which proves the facts and is in turn proved by them, which is circular reasoning *without* any toehold on reality. Lang does not even consider creation as an alternative theory. Although evolution fails to meet the test of a good theory in being able to predict, "it has been very helpful in 'predicting backwards'" (52). Thus Lang, who considers evolution as "fact" and any questioning of it "spurious," is no help in understanding *why* the theory is valid and necessary. Similarly, Cyril Vollert, S. J., in dealing with "Evolution and the Bible," gives us only certain revisions of Biblical thought on the *premise* of evolution, believing "Adam is simply a hypothesis that is admissible but unverifiable" "from the scientific point of view" (115). And this "scientific point of view" now governs Biblical studies in the Roman Church, so that the historicity of Genesis 1-11, "primitive literature," is challenged, the documentary hypothesis embraced, and Scripture treated with the same radical analysis which characterizes modernism; this, moreover, is now presented in the church's appeal to potential converts as evidence that science and Rome are not in conflict. (See the Knights of Columbus Religious Information Bureau pamphlet no. 48, *God's Story of Creation.*)

It becomes apparent, from this quick survey, that neither science nor theology is the source of this acceptance of evolution. It is, clearly, philosophy. Vollert indeed heads his study with the words of Thomas Aquinas, "The ultimate end of the whole process of generation is the human soul, and to it matter tends as toward its final form" (*Contra Gentes*, III, c. 22).

This philosophic basis Andrew G. van Melsen expounds. Indeed, van Melsen is ready to say that macro-evolution is in a sense beyond scientific proof, even if abiogenesis should occur in a laboratory. Moreover, he denies the validity of claims concerning mutation: "the thesis that macro-evolution is caused by the same factors as micro-evolution—namely, random-mutation, selection, and isolation, is for the time being an extrapolation far beyond the realm of experimentally established facts" (62). However, he accepts the validity of the geological time-tables. And evolution is for him a matter of truth whose meaning is better established philosophically than scientifically. To prove or disprove it is not the task of philosophy; it is the congeniality of evolution to the philosophy of the church which he develops.

In answer to attempts to explain the phenomena of life in terms of physics and chemistry, he points out that physics and chemistry cannot adequately explain inanimate nature. However, van Melsen is not ready to see the issue as one between mechanism and vitalism in the sense that one is truth and the other error. This assumes the "deadness" of matter on the part of vitalism and the reduction of life to something lower on the part of mechanism. Instead, "neither biological life nor intellectual life should be conceived as external additions to material being" (72). Higher forms are not higher forms because something new has been added to matter: "they are higher forms because of the unfolding of something already present in matter" (73f.). Evolution is thus "based upon the nature of matter, upon its immanent properties. The course the evolution actually has taken may have been arbitrary and irregular, yet the very existence of the different forms of life shows how these forms are the natural results of the material potencies." Man similarly is a "product of the working of these blind tendencies." "What else should we expect?" (78). Vollert gives us a touching picture of the first human pair, a girl and a boy, born of "a certain anthropoid family," gradually separating themselves from the strong maternal sentiment common to apes and monkeys and leaving the horde to lead a human life (109). Why this first pair were not both of the same sex, or why they chose each other, we are not told. They are allowed to fade into the jungle to build their Eden!

Obviously, in van Melsen's picture there is no place for a fall — only for steady upward movement. Nor is there a concept of sin. Vollert is troubled about this, but is sure that somehow the church will have an answer. Truth and error will apparently lie down together. In van Melsen's scheme, all men are potentially naturally good because of what is inherent in matter, because of their natural potentiality. Sin is underdeveloped structure preventing freedom in goodness. Science must "examine what material structures prevent man from being himself. Perhaps in the long run science will succeed in improving these structures and so open up new possibilities of spiritual life for many people who now partly or wholly are deprived from it." Christ is nowhere to be seen in this picture. After all, what need is there of a Savior to bring redemption to man, or what need of his Second Coming? "Finality, on the human level, therefore, can be considered as the fulfillment of the inherent tendencies of matter, the unfolding of what they are meant to be." The ultimate meaning of matter is found in man, and the importance of evolution is that "it shows the meaning of its (matter's) potencies and tendencies" (79f.).

How is it possible for a church which claims to be Christian to welcome such philosophy, giving it an *imprimatur*, and to allow it rapidly to take command of its thinking? Although Rome has protected itself here as elsewhere by stating that no *ex cathedra* or infallible pronouncement has been made, the *permission* given to evolutionary thinking and the contempt heaped on "fundamentalist" and creationist thinking is more than sufficient indication that *a stand has been made*.

Behind this stand is the incubus of Greek philosophy, now rapidly taking over every aspect of Roman thought. In van Melsen it is clear-cut. The evolutionary picture fits in beautifully with the concept of the *great chain of being*, far more congenially, indeed, than the hostile and alien Biblical doctrine of creation by a sovereign and all-sufficient God. "Matter, as such, is a reduced mode of being because it is devoid of intellectual knowledge and organic life. There is, so to speak, a proportion between the degree of knowledge a being possesses and its degree of being" (72). All the dangers Van Til has pointed out as inherent in Greek thinking, wherever it appears, whether in Roman, Arminian, or supposedly Reformed form, are here spelled out in unmistakable clarity. According to van Melsen, "We are, therefore, entitled to the conclusion that there is a proportion between the degree of knowledge a being possesses and its degree of being" (73). Thus, salvation becomes essentially a greater participation in being, and evolution is a salvation-process whereby the whole material creation grows upward in its possession of or participation in being. There is here no doctrine of creation, fall, or redemption in any inherent or true sense; they must be super-imposed and reinterpreted to have meaning. Vollert is aware of the contradiction:

> The idea of a Fall from a level of perfection possessed from the outset yields to the idea of a level toward which to struggle in the future. Perfection is to be found, not at the beginning of the road, but at the end. These two points of view on human origins are hard to harmonize, and the more the scientific description of early man gains in clarity, the more the picture painted by revelation tends to vanish toward folklore.

> To tell the truth, the man exhibited by the author of Genesis is not the primitive man of Java or Peking, but a man of his own time and nation transported to an idealized version of a garden bearing topographical features of an oasis in his own country. Contemporary theology is well aware of this situation, and is eager to trace out a solution (111).

The Knights of Columbus pamphlet, *God's Story of Creation*, does give us a "solution" to this:

What the author (of the Flood account) is doing by means
of this story, consequently, is to enunciate some rather
profound religious truths, which are transcendent of the
time, the place, and the extent of the Flood which the
story tells about. They would be equally true even if there
were no historical basis to the Flood at all, though we have
good reason to believe in it, quite apart from the Biblical
story (40).

It is clear from this that, *not history, but "ideas" are the basic
reality.* (We are here in the same realm of ideas that neo-
orthodoxy exemplifies.) This is no new philosophy in Rome.
Hear Father Richard W. Grace speak of the sacrifice of Christ
in terms of the agony in the Garden of Gethsemane:

> That Divine High-Priest, who is Truth itself and a priest
> according to the order of Melchisedech, and who had
> really victimized Himself under the appearance of bread
> and wine, thereby unfitted His Body to hold His Blood
> and unfitted His Blood to abide in His Body; and, in
> consequence, unfitted both Body and Blood to continue in
> union with His human soul. [2]

The real sacrifice was not on the Cross, but in the Upper
Room, not so much in the *history* as in the *idea.* The Cross
made the sacrifice in the Upper Room a public act, and fixed
Christ's status as a sacrificial victim. The words, "It is finished"
are thus interpreted: "These words do not declare that His
sacrifice was finished, but that He had finished His former,
normal, earthly life and was now fixed in the state of a victim"
(Grace, 108, cited in Macaulay, 28f.). Again, and more plainly,

> It was not on the Cross that Christ was made a victim. No,
> it was there that He completed His sacrifice both by its
> public manifestation and by finishing His passage from
> His former, normal earthly life into the permanent state of
> a victim.

> In vain would our Divine Lord have come down to save
> us, have been made man in the stable of Bethlehem, have

[2.] R. W. Grace, *The Sacrifice of Christ* (J. F. Wagner, 1937), 75, cited in J.
C. Macaulay, *The Bible and The Roman Church* (Chicago: Moody Press,
1946), 27f.

died for us on the Cross, if He had not left us this Blessed Memorial of His Passion (32-33).

The efficacy of the Cross is thus made to depend on the Supper, of which the mass is the perpetuation. As Macaulay points out, the two great prerogatives of the priesthood, as stated by Cardinal Manning, are "jurisdiction over the natural and over the mystical Body of Christ" [from H. E. Manning, *Eternal Priesthood* (Burns, 1883), 12, cited in Macaulay, 57]. The Cure de 'Ars, J.B.M. Vianney, could say to pilgrims, "See the power of the priest! By one word from his lips, he changes a piece of bread into a God! A greater feat than the creation of a world" (Macaulay, 57). *History* is subordinated to and separated to a degree from the *idea* or *form*, and that idea is incarnated in an institution, the Church of Rome. Thus, the concept of evolution, with its essentially Greek background, is congenial to Rome and thoroughly usable in terms of its basic philosophy. Evil is essentially negation or thinness of being, whereas the good is greater participation in being and a rise in the scale of being. As Van Til has pointed out repeatedly, the compromise of Thomas Aquinas with Greek thought shifted the problem of salvation from ethics to metaphysics.

> Man but stultifies himself if he tries to become eternal. Religious activity as well as ethical activity is always temporal activity. Romanism virtually denies this and evangelicalism all too constantly forgets it (C. Van Til, *Christian Theistic Ethics*, 39).

It is not surprising, in view of these developments, that the doctrine of papal infallibility has been formulated, the concept of tradition developed (so important in terms of the whole developmental and evolutionary idea), and a new doctrine of inspiration set forth. For, in accepting the conclusions of radical higher criticism, Rome has not dropped the concept of Scripture's inspiration and infallibility, reserved now for the idea of Scripture, not its human aspects and accidents. Although "the authors" of the "two accounts" of creation in Genesis were "evidently thinking only in terms of direct creation by God," we must conclude that "between the teaching of the Bible on man and the findings of science, there is no contradiction whatever." The *idea* in both stories, briefly, is that "man is different." "Genesis neither proves nor disproves the theory of evolution. It simply does not consider it at all. Neither does science prove or disprove the religious doctrine taught by Genesis. These do not pertain to the scope of positive science" (*God's Story of Creation*, 20-23. See also Knights of Columbus, *The Infallible Church, Truth or Trickery?* pamphlet no. 56). On the one hand, a radical unity of all being is asserted in the chain of being concept; on the other hand, to prevent the destruction of all values by the total relativity the oneness of being posits, history and idea are separated. The historicity of the idea becomes irrelevant. The question again resolves itself into philosophy.

How can this doctrine of Biblical inspiration and infallibility be best described? The Vatican Council thus defined papal infallibility:

> When he (the Pope) speaks *ex cathedra*, that is, when, in fulfilling his office as supreme shepherd and teacher of all Christians, by virtue of his supreme Apostolic authority, he defines a doctrine concerning faith or morals to be held by the whole Church, he enjoys that same infallibility with which our Divine Redeemer willed His Church to be endowed in defining doctrine pertaining to faith and morals.

This same doctrine of infallibility is in essence now read back into Scripture: it is the essence, the idea, that is protected from error. Even as the pope cannot speak infallibly on matters of history or science and is not preserved from personal sin, but is made infallible in his teaching power in doctrines pertaining to faith and morals, so the inspiration and infallibility of the Biblical writers is similarly viewed. This is in essence not too different from the recent statement of an ostensibly Reformed leader: "I recognize and admit no errors, inaccuracies, contradictions, or other inadequacies of any sort in Scripture which affect its authority on this, its message." Here is a radical separation of the realm of nature (history) and the realm of ethics and religion (idea), the one being open to scientific inquiry and subject to error and change, the other being beyond inquiry and eternal and free. This is increasingly the approach, since Kant, of vast segments of Protestantism, as well as of Rome. Although the two worlds are linked in various artificial ways, and the world of ideas given a hierarchical priority, the division between the two grows steadily in modern religious thought. And with it, the irrelevance of such religion to the world of history grows more conspicuous. The tendency of all such thinking is the same—the apotheosis of man. And our judgment of all such must be God's judgment, as expressed by Paul, in speaking of men "who changed the truth of God into a lie and worshipped and served the creature more than the Creator, who is blessed for ever. Amen" (Rom. 1:25).

Scripture Index

Index

The Author

Rousas John Rushdoony (1916-2001) was a well-known American scholar, writer, and author of over thirty books. He held B.A. and M.A. degrees from the University of California and received his theological training at the Pacific School of Religion. An ordained minister, he worked as a missionary among Paiute and Shoshone Indians as well as a pastor to two California churches. He founded the Chalcedon Foundation, an educational organization devoted to research, publishing, and cogent communication of a distinctively Christian scholarship to the world at large. His writing in the *Chalcedon Report* and his numerous books spawned a generation of believers active in reconstructing the world to the glory of Jesus Christ. He resided in Vallecito, California until his death, where he engaged in research, lecturing, and assisting others in developing programs to put the Christian Faith into action.

The Ministry of Chalcedon

CHALCEDON (kal•see•don) is a Christian educational organization devoted exclusively to research, publishing, and cogent communication of a distinctively Christian scholarship to the world at large. It makes available a variety of services and programs, all geared to the needs of interested ministers, scholars, and laymen who understand the propositions that Jesus Christ speaks to the mind as well as the heart, and that His claims extend beyond the narrow confines of the various institutional churches. We exist in order to support the efforts of all orthodox denominations and churches. Chalcedon derives its name from the great ecclesiastical Council of Chalcedon (A.D. 451), which produced the crucial Christological definition: "Therefore, following the holy Fathers, we all with one accord teach men to acknowledge one and the same Son, our Lord Jesus Christ, at once complete in Godhead and complete in manhood, truly God and truly man...." This formula directly challenges every false claim of divinity by any human institution: state, church, cult, school, or human assembly. Christ alone is both God and man, the unique link between heaven and earth. All human power is therefore derivative: Christ alone can announce that "All power is given unto me in heaven and in earth" (Matthew 28:18). Historically, the Chalcedonian creed is therefore the foundation of Western liberty, for it sets limits on all authoritarian human institutions by acknowledging the validity of the claims of the One who is the source of true human freedom (Galatians 5:1).

The *Chalcedon Report* is published monthly and is sent to all who request it. All gifts to Chalcedon are tax deductible.

Chalcedon
Box 158
Vallecito, CA 95251 U.S.A.
www.chalcedon.edu

CPSIA information can be obtained at www.ICGtesting.com
Printed in the USA
BVOW071348080513

320188BV00003B/864/A